Sanguine-Love

An incredible story with a practical guide
on how to overcome life´s challenges

Iva Schubart

For any queries
email: iva@ivaschubart.com
Website: www.ivaschubart.com

First printing: June 2018
Printed in India

ISBN: 978-93-87269-62-0
Cover Design : Team StoryMirror

STORYMIRROR
Stories that reflect you

Publisher: **StoryMirror Infotech Pvt. Ltd.**
1108, 11th floor Pragati Tower, Rajendra Place,
New Delhi-110008.
145, First Floor, Powai Plaza,
Hiranandani Gardens,
Powai - 400076, Mumbai, India

Web:	www.storymirror.com
Facebook:	www.facebook.com/storymirror
Twitter:	https://twitter.com/story_mirror
Instagram:	https://instagram.com/storymirror

Acknowledgment

I am so grateful for the love from my family. All my friends and the spiritual teachers whose guidance led me to accomplish this book.

To my family and friends:

My father František, who taught me with his intellect and humour on how to be adventurous, forever looking for the next step, no matter what happens. He left his mortal body in 2002 but his spirit is still with me.

My mother Miluše, who was the seed for my own transformational path after giving me the Czech version of "Living with joy" from Sanaya Roman, 20 years ago. I read the very same book in English during my transformational program in 2015. Without knowing I have had the Czech version of this book on my shelves for more than 20 years. I always knew our souls are unconditionally connected. Her words, "Ivanka, I only want you to be happy", became a reality. Mum I love you, you will be always in my soul.

She left her body in 2017.

My older sister Jana, who will not only watch over me as a doctor, but she is my best friend as well, even though we live far away from each other and have different point of view.

Our bond strengthened after my mother passed away in the summer of 2017. We are both facing and were faced with the challenges of living and making a career abroad.

My older brother Milan, who is always there for me, his younger sister. His helpful heart, taking care of our mother for the last few years of her life in Brno. I truly thank him for his incredible support. A big bow to him.

My older daughter Zaira, who teaches me with her free, adventurous and intelligent spirit and strength how to follow your dream even though there are hurdles on the way. She teaches me how to overcome them.

My youngest daughter Natalie, who is my mirror. Her intelligence, humour and extra ordinary sportive character that make a lot of people adore her like a friend and leader as well.

My grandmother Růžena Mašin, who taught me to play the piano and from whom I inherited a beautiful voice.

My grandfather Emil Ondryáš, who taught me to be adventurous and courageous.

My dearest friend, Leon, I am grateful for all your qualities and the way you show your love to me, structuring and supporting me in the realisation of my book even when we went through tough times together.

My sparring friend, Paul, for his verbal knowledge, to rephrase my words in this book and to keep me accountable.

My friend Wim, who always helped and helps me during my challenging times and times of transformation.

To all my spiritual teachers and authors who have been a guidance for me in realising my book. Among them I want to mention:

Christy Whitman – for me, the number one law of attraction coach who led me to take her program. She was the starting point of my transformation.

Esther and Jerry Hicks – Ask and it is given – learning to manifest the Law of attraction.

Louise Hay – her teaching on mirror work and her books taught me a lot on how to start within yourself.

Robert Holden – whom I met during the writers' workshop in Bristol and who was an inspiration for me with his book, "Life loves you" and his teachings on success.

Eckhart Thole – his book, "New earth" that opened my eyes on the very beginning of my path.

Deepak Chopra – whose knowledge and spiritual guidance is phenomenal. His book "The 7 spiritual laws of success" is one that I truly recommend.

Sanaya Roman – especially her book, "Living with joy", which my mother gave me 20 years ago. Without knowing I would reach out for this book after 20 years and to take learnings from it during my transformational path – here is where the law of attraction and my journey to the destination started.

Joseph Campbell – his teaching on "The journey of the hero".

Wallace D. Wattles – his book, "Science of getting rich".

Neal Donald Walsch – his teaching on "Conversations with God".

Joe Dispenza – his book, "Evolve your brain".

Wayne Dyer – his movie and teachings - "The shift".

Marianne Williamson – her book and teachings – "A return to love".

I dedicate this book to all these and other spiritual teachers for their guidance to start living in joy, happiness and freedom.

"One´s real life is so often the life one does not lead."

- Oscar Wilde

Preface

Yes, I did it! I have written my first book.

My mother would be so proud.

Maybe more books will follow, who knows?

I am delighted with the result. I do hope you will enjoy it as well. Moreover, it is my goal to support you in your journey by writing down my own life story; the story of a Czech girl. The story of the first 50 years of my life. I would like to think of those 50 years as an extension to my childhood.

A childhood of joy, love and bliss. But also, a childhood of severe pain, abuse, disappointment, setbacks and sorrow. I will show you what I have learned from that very same childhood, what I have discovered and what transformed me into the sanguine person I turned into. I will show you how great a human being already is and how we loose track of it. I will show you what I have learned from the greatest teachers in the world. So much to show you. I promise you, I present to you only the most valuable treasures.

You know, there are a lot of self-help books out there. There is so much to learn and to choose from. It looks like 'Walhalla', but sometimes it leaves you confused as to which path or guideline to choose from. This book is not a book to give you the complete outline in becoming a self-loving human. There is no right path or one way to get where you want to be.

This book will present to you a unique story and specific tips that are derived from that story. Tips that direct you in a subtle way. Tips on self-love. It may lead to new insights coming from deep inside of you. These insights are your guides, your own personal guide. Cherish them. Unwrap them like precious presents. You might find one on each page and if not, turn to the next page. You will find your own, I am sure of it.

These insights will turn your life upside down. In a safe way, do not worry...

They will guide you away from fear. They will guide you to self-love. Sanguine love. They will cause vibrations inside of you. People will recognise these vibrations. The vibrations will attract people and opportunities with the same vibrations. Magical things will start to happen. Synchronicity will appear. Life will become much easier and happier.

At first some of the insights will require challenging work though. You will need to break through the walls of fear. Sometimes your effort will show you just that, what you may have known all the time and you will instantly know what to do. Just like that. Sometimes you will be asked to do something in order to feel or transform yourself. And sometimes you can choose to do an exercise that may feel weird at first but in the long run it will free you from the undesired part you were playing.

Let the learning from this book fully embrace you. Let the book guide you to sanguine-love. Let the book inspire you. Let the book cause vibrations you may have never felt before. Let the book attract you to a whole new world full of possibilities.

I wrote this book in remembrance of my mother. After she died I promised her and myself to write this book. A book about how she could have written herself since she loved to write. It is a book about how self-love can be re-discovered. The self-love my mother was not able to discover herself, unfortunately.

Still, she is my true inspiration, my spiritual teacher, my soul mate. She is like a lighthouse. Every time I need a message, some signal, she will be there. Let me be your lighthouse now. The only thing you should do is to look in the right direction every now and then. I will be there and you can count on it.

My light will shine for you. Let it see you in the spotlight. Your very own spotlight.

Introduction

I wanted to be an artist once upon a time.

Now I am an artist. It took me fifty years.

I was born in Egypt, raised in the Czech Republic and I then migrated to the Netherlands. This book captures the precious insights from my personal journey through these countries and my transformation after I turned fifty. I like to think of myself as the Czech girl living in the Netherlands with a Bohemian perspective, offering a practical guide on how to overcome life's challenges. My motivation in all this is to show how it is possible to change and transform your life, whether you are fifty, above or under fifty or beyond menopause. Finding true sanguine-love is the core theme of this book.

For your readability, the book is divided into several chapters which have been divided into two major sections – my past life and my life after fifty.

The section 'My past life' contains chapters about my personal experiences which are combined with insights into these experiences and are concluded with exercises, reflections and a conclusion. Main chapters in this section include 'Born in Egypt', 'My Birth', 'Moving to the Czech-Republic', 'My Experience with Communism', 'The Rag Doll Purpose' and 'A Traumatic Experience'. Other chapters are 'The Emigration to the Netherlands' and 'Married life'.

The second section of the book are chapters under the section 'Life After 50' with valuable exercises. These exercises are the best out there. How do I know? A lot of people benefited from them since they have been presented by the best teachers out there. Teachers like Wayne Dyer, Louise Hay, Thich Nath Hanh and many others.

The focus of each chapter in this section includes self-development, knowing who you are and what you want, self-love, finding purpose, finding your soul mate, better sex after fifty, how to be happier, how to be healthier, how to be successful, how to be wealthier and several spiritual/universal laws.

Let me make one thing clear. I do not want you to make a big study out of this book. I want you to be inspired. I want you to feel something. I want you to discover something. But whatever you do or want to be, make up your own mind. Even better, feel the power of your sanguine-love. Enjoy it.

Eventually, when you take a close look in the mirror; you will love your wrinkles, you will love the colour of your eyes, you will love your radiance, you will love your smile, will fall in love with all your imperfections, you will love your navel even if it is buried in your belly, because you love all your imperfections. And you know what, you will see the world around you in the same way. You will see a goldmine in everyone out there.

I wish you a lot of gold. And if you find it, let me know.

Iva

Contents

MY PAST LIFE

Chapter I

Egypt and my birth

We have gravity to blame because gravity is pushing us down
That is why we are not free and cannot fly.
Still, we desire to fly and use our wings
Up to the sky and beyond.
Let's keep trying and trying,
Never ever give up.

- Iva Schubart

In 1964, my whole family moved to Cairo, Egypt. My father had already been working there for the past one and a half year. He was a researcher and professor at the technical military university. The funny part of it is, that I was not even born in that year. However, I still consider us moving to Egypt as the first step in my life, since being born in that country under the circumstances we would live in and the events that would happen, would have such a great lasting impact on my life. One year later I was born. Yes, Iva was there.

The night I was born was a sultry one. It was a really hot night. Locals believed these nights to be mysterious and fairy-like, as if a mystical thing would happen. It was the 18th of June, 1965.

My father was not aware that something extraordinary was

about to take place. He had taken off to dreamland. You could not have woken him up even with the sounds of the most ear-splitting fireworks. My mother, however, was fully awake and aware because she was experiencing severe pains from the contractions. She was very nervous, on the edge of being anxious, which was quite understandable because she had already suffered two miscarriages in the past.

She did whatever she could to wake my father up; shouting, screaming, clapping her hands, nothing worked. My father was clearly exhausted because of the long and intensive hours at work. He was still breathing, fortunately, while being completely clocked out.

My brother and sister were playing upstairs in the living room, unaware of what was going on. They even found the predicament of my mother funny and entertaining, because of all the 'silly' noises she was making. In the meantime, they were, of course, oblivious to the meaning of what was going on.

The pain did not disappear or become less. Whatever my mother tried, nothing worked. She was forced to call a taxi. At that time, it was already 3 o'clock at night and the pain had intensified. The contractions came every 10 minutes now, being a clear sign, the delivery would start real soon. As the taxi arrived she tried to 'hurry' herself to the elevator. Finally, she got in. I do not know how it happened, but suddenly in some way, my father had woken up and had found his way to the elevator as well. They got in to the cab and rushed through busy Cairo. Even at those hours Cairo is busy. It is always crowded. Never asleep, like a metropolis.

On the way to the hospital my mother remarkably had the presence of mind to even find some time to dream between the twinges of pain. *'Would it be a girl or a boy?'* she wondered.

In those days, ultrasound imaging did not exist, hence the gender of a child remained a mystery and was always a wonderful surprise; a highly treasured moment for most families. It was not different for my parents.

At the hospital everyone spoke French. Mostly French-speaking patients visited the hospital as the hospital took care of most of the people in the community of French diplomats in the local area. My mother was the only Czech woman in Egypt to give birth. She and my father both spoke French.

They immediately took care of her. Her labour did not take long and luckily with far less pain than she had suffered back home. The moment had arrived. While my father had to sit and wait outside, because in those days men were not allowed to witness, let alone support their wives at childbirth. The nurse encouraged my mother in her last efforts to deliver.

'Allez, pousse et pousse encore une peu!'; ('Come on, come on, push and push some more').

And there I was. At the very moment the sun showed its face on the horizon. Iva was born!

The medical staff at the hospital were in awe over my hair. Since my sister and brother were both blond, I was the exception. I had very dark, luscious, full head of hair. They even went as far as the thought that I had mistakenly been mixed-up with another baby in the ward. Luckily, I wore a hospital bracelet with my mother's name on it; Miluše. My sister came up with my name; Ivanka, named after her favourite doll. My parents supported it.

And so, this is how it all started. The wonderful sunrise of the journey of my life.

The Universal Law of Seeds

To embrace the law of seeds is to embrace the will to keep trying and trying until we succeed.

The Law of Seeds[1]

Reflecting on my birth and the miscarriages my mother had to experience, I envision a personal journey I had taken even before I was born. The pain my parents had to suffer, and the effort in my birth is a part of who and what I am today. There is a universal law exhibited by my parents and therefore by me; The Law of Seeds.

Let me illustrate the meaning of this law with the following metaphor.

Think about an orange tree for a second. One tree may have a dozen fruits and in turn, each single fruit may have up to ten seeds. You might wonder, why so many seeds in a fruit when only one or two may become a beautiful tree full of new oranges?

In that question itself lies the answer: not all seeds grow into what they are supposed to become.

The human journey in fact begins with the release of 100 million semen. However, only one sperm cell in these vast numbers manages to penetrate the ovary and fertilization occurs.

Not every seed is a success and the same thing counts for our lives. To realise our dreams, or to reach a certain goal, we must embrace the willingness to try again and again and again.

My mother would have had a good reason to stop trying for another child after two miscarriages. I never would have been born.

You often observe this law in everyday life. Thousands of

1. *Based on the book "The Law of Seeds" - Sampson Amoateng*

contestants may compete in a competition but there is only one winner who wins all; over fifty people hunt for that one job and are assessed for that one job but only one person gets it; after sending out hundreds of marketing letters, you may get that one subscriber that changes everything.

To embrace the Law of Seeds is to embrace the willingness to keep trying until we succeed. When we adopt this law, we take failure or flaws less personal and find renewed energy and motivation to pursue our goals in life.

The rag doll purpose

Like almost every child I too owned a small rag doll. I considered this doll as the one and only entity that would never leave me. Like the perfect loved one, most beloved one, the doll always allowed me unlimited squeezing and kissing privileges. Who else would grant that?

I called her Ivanka as well. Is it possible that this doll was something of an omen that made me write this book after all these years?

My mother did not want me to play with Barbie dolls. She asserted that Barbie dolls looked like naked women and it was therefore not appropriate for children to play with them. Yes, my mother had her mysterious ways as well. As a child, my mother's decision did not make sense to me, but later, as I grew older, I came to understand her perspective. And so, I had this plain but precious doll with no clearly distinguishable feminine features.

One day, when I was about three years old and I still remember it vividly as I had my first fight with a boy. He too was about three or four years old. I think he was from Nigeria. We lived in a neighbourhood full of people from several countries, expatriates' living in a separate community. We were playing outside with a lot of other children, like we did most of the time, and he wanted my doll. I refused to give it to him and we took to struggling over the doll that led to a fight, all at the same time. I was quite strong despite my tiny frame, so I fought and fought. My head turned red, my hands and arms soured but he did not succeed in taking my doll. Unfortunately, the doll was ruined. I got a piece of her body, arms and legs and the boy got the head. Can you imagine how that made me feel? My sweet loved one destroyed. I was devastated, and I rushed back home, in the hope of being comforted by my mother.

Our nanny stumbled out to meet me.

'*What happened?*', she demanded. '*What's going on?*'

My mother was not at home at that moment as she was out swimming. The nanny gave me some soda to calm me down. While gasping and sobbing, I stuttered through my story. My brother stood by puzzled about so much to do about nothing. At least that is what he thought. It was written all over his face.

Reflection

In our childhood, our purpose and desires are so pure and focused. We know how to stand up for ourselves because we clearly know what is important to us. Just like that and never even thinking about it. It is just so clear to us. Intuitively. For me at that point, my poppy doll was my purpose and desire. That is why I fought so doggedly for it and was so devastated when it was ruined.

However, it seems that when we grow up, we lose this sense of purpose and clarity about what we really want because we do not stand up for our own truth anymore. We are afraid to fight for what we believe in. And I ask myself: '*Why is this so?*'

Maybe it is because we are no longer seekers searching for answers, but we are more like hunted animals. The society patronises our personal desires, frowns on our individuality and forces us to conform to norms and live a life we really do not want, desire or understand. We stop playing, exploring, wondering and start grating on the inside. We become like sheep that never ever leave their flock and only make a lot of noise when we think we are deprived of our fundamental rights and needs for food, sex, sleep, job, a home, some nice children and a big fat wallet.

I was also once part of that 'conformist' crowd, right up to when I turned fifty. Then I got a deep insight: now or never is the time to shine, to become my absolute best, giving light and direction to people especially the ones that are lost while living in their flock.

If we can rediscover that which was never really lost, that magic of childhood, where our purpose and determination is pure and makes us feel blissful, we will create a world of our own desires. In that world, we do what we truly want to do rather than being boxed into something we do not want to do or be someone we are not. It's possible for everyone. Each human can live a liberated life, a fulfilling life.

Conclusion

My 'Why' to write this book became instantly clear after the death of my mother in 2017. It fuelled my desire to share my story of traumas, change and transformations. I suddenly knew these stories could inspire thousands of people to understand their own purpose or 'Why'. A 'Why' that breathes passion in everything you do, doing everything with greater purpose and therefore focus and enthusiasm.

In the next story, in which I experienced that blissfulness, that magic of my childhood, that purity. Even more, I am sure you will recognise this because you undoubtedly had similar experiences also.

The camel ride in 1968

"We can only derive intense enjoyment from a contrast and only very little from a state of things"

- *Sigmund Freud* [2]

The first few years of my life were very happy. Egypt had and still has a very nice warm climate and we could swim all year round. What more could a child ask for? I loved to play and swim in our very own luxury pool. Even at three years old, I could already swim well. I swam like a fish in the water. I sincerely believe that in those years I built my perseverance and inner strength by spending so much time exercising and playing in the water.

Straight diving, cannonball diving, staying under water for as long as I could while holding my breath, tumbling and turning under water, I tried a lot of things including trying to do the front crawl, back crawl and butterfly stroke, lap after lap. 'The Universal Law of Seeds' of trying and trying and trying until I succeeded was nurtured by me, unconsciously, even at that age.

I also enjoyed those years because we, as a family could do all the things we loved since money was not an issue. We lived in luxury because my dad had a very respectable job.

One day we went for a camel ride near the pyramids. I was thrilled. In those days this was a real adventure. There were no tourists back then. No souvenir shops what so ever. It was a mystical place. A place of unspoiled nature, a place to amaze oneself about the miracle of people building these magnificent pyramids, a place where you could even find fossils and artefacts straight at your feet. It was like shopping

2. *Sigmund Freud (1856-1939) was an Austrian neurologist and the founder of psychoanalysis, a clinical method for treating psychopathology through dialogue between a patient and a psychoanalyst.*

for free in a huge candy store. I found a beard of a small Pharaoh statue.

Most of the time I looked around with great awe. I heard the Arabs speaking their inconceivable language. It all made a deep impact on me and I really felt at home in this mystical place. If you could have seen me then you would probably laugh about my eyes almost being popped out of my head from seeing such superb splendour everywhere around me. The huge ice cream with soda (I got the biggest one since I was the youngest) made it special.

That mystical experience brought a big smile on my face. Could this be heaven? Years later I realised this was the very first moment I felt complete, pure and totally comfortable. A kind of blissful feeling came over me, sitting on that camel high above the sand, my brother holding me firmly. I was wearing a short skirt and a nice white blouse with puffed sleeves; the wind and sun nurturing my skin. I was the princess of the desert. The queen of the universe.

Chapter II

One-way ticket back to Czechoslovakia and communism

The struggle of man against power is the struggle of memory against forgetting.

- *Milan Kundera* [3]

Summer 1969, Departure from Egypt

August 1969: my parents are restless, we were about to depart back to Czechoslovakia. Back to our homeland.

It is necessary to tell you this story of our departure from Egypt, as you will then be able to understand how history influenced the mood and behaviour of my parents and me. Could you even imagine what an enormous impact the Soviet indoctrination can have on people's life? For our family, it destroyed the career of my father, it affected our sense of individuality, our autonomy, our feeling of being alive and our sense of having purpose and meaning.

My father had a prominent position at the military technical university. He was one of the leading people at that university, often consulted by high civil servants and government officials. The research

3. *Milan Kundera (1929) was a Czech novelist, author of "The book of laughter and forgetting" and his father was my mother's piano teacher*

that was conducted and led by my father, was of very high importance. Because of his position he was close to President Nasser and Prime Minister Mubarak who later became president of Egypt after Nasser died in 1970.

Those constructive and friendly relationships were not much appreciated by the Czech diplomat who represented Czechoslovakia in Egypt. The Czech diplomat was Russian by origin. He was a former Russian soldier who had worked his way up with almost no education what so ever. He was clearly envious of my dad because of his intelligence, position and most of all his strong relationships with Nasser and Mubarak.

The diplomat surrounded my dad with colleagues who were supposed to gather information about my father's activities, especially anything that could be discovered about my father's contacts with the president. These so-called colleagues also envied my father for his position and the benefits that came with the job. They gladly spied for the diplomat.

Moreover, Nasser and his successor Sadat were not real pro-Russian presidents. Therefore, the diplomat grabbed each opportunity to make it difficult for my father to do his job.

My father was not the most diplomatic person you can imagine. He was straight, pure, honest and bright. He stated his opinions openly with vigour. As a democratic he disliked oppression of any kind. However, he never desired to become politically active nor had he ever been in that arena.

Still anything that he said that could be used against him was gathered. He was even accused of being a spy because he planned foreign trips regularly. My father loved to travel. He even started his own travel agency for his fellow Czechs who lived in Egypt. They were all well-educated and bright. It was a large group of about one hundred friends and expats.

Complete families, friends and colleagues travelled in a bus to discover beautiful new foreign places. My father always loved to take my sister on these trips, so he could give her a worldlier view. Later my sister assured me that during these trips she was always near my father. My dad never left her alone. Never ever did my father have any strange encounters with others during these trips talking about so-called state sensitive secrets. However, these trips were considered to be suspicious by the Czech diplomat.

Only a few months later he lost his job. The job he loved. The job in which he performed well, the job he was praised for by so many. Hence, we were forced to return to Czechoslovakia in August 1969.

One year earlier, on the 21st of August 1968 to be precise, the Russians had occupied Czechoslovakia. This meant the end of the 'Prague Spring', a period of major reformation. A reformation to turn our beloved country in a social nation with a human face, led by Dubček, our popular prime minister. A nation, free of oppression, made my father ever so proud. However, this period was harshly ended by the Soviet occupation. My father turned real sad and disillusioned because of this. The very thought of being ruled by the Soviets, guided by their oppressing ideology was unbearable and unacceptable for my father.

It reminds me of the movie 'The Unbearable Lightness of Being[4]*. It is based on a novel by Milan Kundera . It follows the lives of two women, two men and a dog during the Prague Spring period in 1968. The movie explores the idea of 'emptiness and meaning', 'lightness and heaviness' in the escapades and adventures of two couples. The movie made an ever-lasting imprint in my heart. I am sure it will impress you as well.*

My father felt a deep urge to return to his beloved country. To support his family and other relatives.

Hence, my mother, brother, my sister and I returned to Czechoslovakia. We travelled by plane. My father and two of his friends drove all the way back in his favourite Skoda 100, which we nicknamed

---

4. *The Unbearable Lightness of Being (Czech: Nesnesitelná lehkost bytí) is a 1984 novel by Milan Kundera. He is a Czech-born French writer who went into exile in France in 1975. Prior to the Velvet Revolution of 1989, the Communist regime in Czechoslovakia banned his books.*

'the blue one', Crossing no less than seven countries; Israel, Lebanon, Syria, Turkey, Bulgaria, Yugoslavia and Austria.

One of his friends quoted a nice anecdote after they arrived safely in Czechoslovakia. During their trip they lost track of their route somewhere in Turkey. In those days you had to navigate with poor out-dated maps. In the middle of the night they could not figure out where they were. They were totally lost. Hence my dad pounded on several doors of some houses in nowhere land. He shouted; *'Open Sesame!'* Nothing happened, the doors stayed closed.

They were forced to put up their tent right where they were at that moment to get some sleep. When they woke up, they realised they had slept in the middle of a town square. All kinds of animals and people of that small rural village were surrounding them. Curious as to why there was a tent in the middle of their town square.

As soon as we landed in Czechoslovakia I saw the devastation in my mother's eyes. That devastation would not leave her until she died in 2017. The great life in Egypt was over, it was definitive, no point of return. It was all over.

Several weeks later when my father arrived, I saw that same look in his eyes. A dear friend of his, who also travelled with him from Egypt to Czechoslovakia, told me the story of crossing the border to Czechoslovakia. My father must have stood there for about one hour. Staring, considering whether to cross or not. Being in a twist, he finally said; *'We have families out there, so let's go!'*

The soldier at the border opened the barrier, even though he did not understand why people wanted to cross the border into Czechoslovakia. He shouted; *'What do you think you can do out here?'* He could not believe they would even consider going into a country where travelling abroad was forbidden. Where they would practically live in a prison with no intellectual freedom whatsoever.

Before my father left Egypt, he got a new job offer in Switzerland, however my mother did not want their parents to suffer on their own. She felt their parents needed all the support they could get. Especially in such a traumatised country. So my dad refused the job offer. That sense of being utterly disappointed combined with the daily confrontation with Russians occupants made it all even worse.

Hence the Czech tragedy and psychological trauma had begun. For all the Czechs including our family. It affected us our entire lives.

Our first president of Czechoslovakia T.G. Masaryk once said so aptly:

'Why did the Habsburg Empire put us between the Soviet Union and Germany?'

Is it not a good question for anybody to fully grasp the significance of this event in Czech history? Like a country being squeezed between two countries known for their oppression.

Life in Czechoslovakia

My mother started looking for a job. She was forty-two. She got a job at a high school, as a teacher in the German language and later in Russian as well. But the devastation remained. Living in an inhumane, communistic society with no freedom whatsoever was unbearable.

I was four years old and living my own ignorant life while my brother and my sister experienced their own adolescent identity search. My father pulled himself back in his own world of thoughts closing himself off from us emotionally. My father who once was at the top of the world, now was unexpectedly lying on the floor feeling knocked out.

All his doctoral books were banned. And worse, his professor title was taken away from him as well. All this happened within a matter of days from crossing the border.

But he never gave up. He was still a fighter, right up to the end. He started a trial, he was the only Czech who started a trial (other Czechs were too scared to stand up and fight for their rights), against his dismissal and he hired a lawyer. The trial was against the leaders of the technical military university in Brno. His lawyer admitted that my father was right and sure to win the lawsuit. However, he had to pull back from defending my father because he was afraid that an action such as this would inevitably harm his own career. A lot of people lived in fear in a society dominated by the Soviets and their inhumane ideology.

Perhaps, have you seen the film 'The Matrix[5]? It demonstrates cinematically the zombie like nature of people being oppressed. The main character (Neo) was offered a choice, to be born again and face reality or to remain a slave and live in ignorance. We never had that

---

5. *The Matrix is a 1999 science fiction action film written and directed by The Wachowskis and starring a/o Keanu Reeves and Laurence Fishburne.*

choice to begin with, living in such harsh circumstances. The Czechs were numbed, everywhere you looked you saw grey faces with no expression at all. Being slaves of a system, in which you had to colour between-the-lines. Crossing those lines meant being punished, unjustly so. Individuality was killed as everyone was forced to conform to the systems dictated by the government and its body. It got to the point of being enslaved in doing whatever you were told to do under the guise of the greater good. And yet, we all were constantly being aware of the brutal consequences if we did not follow. This is a system annihilating all human creativity, autonomy, self-direction and liberty.

An infamous illustration is the story about the amazing Czech singer, Marta Kubišová. She had an incredible voice, so bright, so much range. She was very popular in the Prague Spring in 1968, especially with her song 'Modlitba pro Martu' (pray for Martha). Her career was crushed by the communists. They threatened to punish her with imprisonment if she dared ever to sing again. It was only after the Velvet Revolution, twenty years later in 1989, she was able to pick-up her career again.

One of the consequences was that my father lost most of his so-called friends and colleagues who were dear to him. The people who loved to make those trips with him. They too had to face total oppression. They too kept silent, too afraid to speak up or choose to live a life they desired. To stand ground and to stay firm for what they believed.

After two years my father found a new lawyer. Upon studying his case he too refused to defend my father due to the political sensitivity. The new president Husák had just launched a new motto; *'Proletarians of all countries connect!'* Which simply meant that each Czech was solely seen as an instrument of labour. Even worse, as a cog in a machine.

Distinction of age, education, background and sex became less important. Everyone was forced to comply with being a proletarian. My father was even ordered to work in a factory as a stoker. You can imagine how humiliating this was for my father, being highly educated. But most of all, because of the insanity of the rule. Putting people down like this. Abusing the potential of people. And yet, he had the courage to refuse.

In those years we lived a moderate life, able to buy only the necessities. No luxury of any kind. Living off of the meagre salary my mother earned. And the little savings we had gathered back in Egypt.

My father became depressed, more and more with every passing day. All this affected his health little by little and he was eventually diagnosed with diabetes. His depressed condition continued for almost seven years until he somehow found the energy to build a new house for us in Brno. That project was his salvation. It healed him.

Reflection

After the death of my mother in 2017, I started the big search. The search for information about my father's life. I looked and searched everywhere. In the online and offline archives of universities, justice departments, ministries, libraries and so on. I travelled to several cities. I spoke with many people, met several old friends of my father, but nobody could give me any clear answers to my questions. I simply wanted to know who my father had really been.

I could not acquire any documents of his legal proceedings in 1970 and 1971, I could not find any evidence why he lost his position knowing he was unjustly punished by the political situation at that time. The only thing I found were some letters and some information of the people who had punished him. The rest was all destroyed. It became clear to me that they wanted the truth to be buried with him.

In 1989 my father was officially rehabilitated. He was allowed to teach again at the university, but at the age of sixty-three, he was unable to do so anymore. A few years before he had picked up a new hobby; collecting stamps. He even started a club of stamp collectors and was known for his extensive knowledge of stamps. At that time the collecting of stamps was very popular. Certain stamps were expensive and sometimes a rare commodity. He also had picked up some work in translating and interpreting technical documentation. In 2002 he died, his body and mind being exhausted from all the suffering he had endured in his life.

Conclusion

In my first fifty years of 'childhood', my life was dominated by a lot of wrong beliefs from my past and by a lot of wrong behavioural patterns. My parents were okay with me having hobbies like singing and performing on stage in the theatre, but they always assured me that to be successful it was necessary to study. Being an actress was not accepted as a serious vocation. It had the certainty of an insecure existence. So, they forced me to go to a technical university. Something I absolutely did not like to do. I had artistic talents and a keen ear for linguistics. Do you recognise similar patterns for yourself? You can imagine that if you have a lot of things in your life that you do not like to do, you will integrate that dislike into your system, your mind, your body, your habits, your choices, and in your behaviour. Subconsciously being taught the wrong standards, values and rules ultimately resulted in connections in the brain that were hard to remove or to be replaced by new ones. It takes some effort. A lot of blood, sweat and tears. But rest assured, it is worth it.

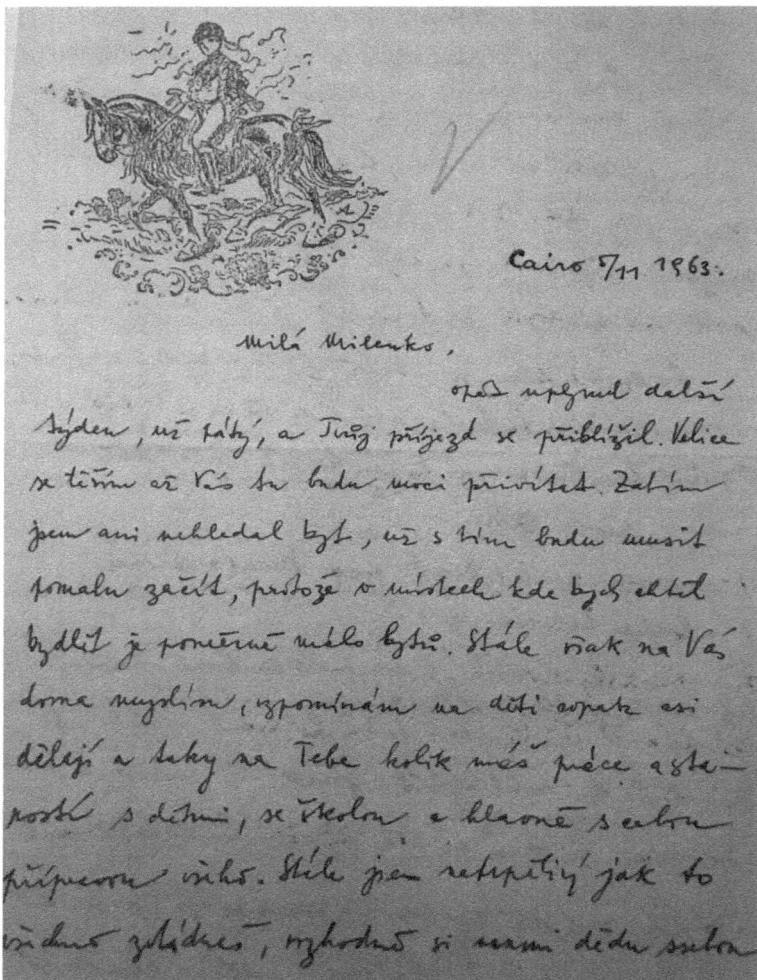

This is one of many letters my father wrote to my mother, during his time in being on his own for a year and a half in Egypt. In every letter, my father expressed his deepest love for my mother and his desire to be with her.

Translation:

'Dearest Milenka' (my father called my mother mistress because of her name Miluše)

(Cairo, November 1963)

(letter 53) 'It is now five weeks prior to you arriving to Egypt. I am looking forward to welcoming you here, the whole family, our children. What do you think, will they still recognise me? I must find a new apartment for us. Luckily there are a few apartments in Cairo where I want to live. I am thinking about you and the children all the time, wondering how you are doing. If you have a tough time working at school, or with the children or with all the preparations for your emigration to Egypt on your own, just know I will always be there for you...'

In a moment of decision, the best thing you can do
is the right thing to do.
The worst thing you can do is do nothing.

- Theodore Roosevelt [6]

A traumatic experience in 1977

When I was twelve years old, I used to go to my grandmother's piano class. My grandmother, an elderly lady, was a former opera singer. She was now a piano teacher who wanted me to learn to play the piano to the best of my ability. Piano lessons on the grand piano with my grandmother was something I always looked forward to. I also enjoyed singing in a children's choir. After auditioning for this choir, I was chosen. They even compared me with a nightingale. Music was so important to me.

On that grand piano stood a statue of a Dutch milk maid ('Die Holländerin') that reminded my grandmother of her half uncle from the Netherlands. Now the same statue is in my living room in the Netherlands. The statue reminds me of my grandmother just like

---

6. *Theodore Roosevelt was an American statesman and writer who served as President of the United States from 1901 to 1909.*

it reminded my grandmother of her half uncle. I always wanted to have that statue. It is amazing to consider the fact that I already had a family relative in the Netherlands, long before I even moved to the Netherlands myself.

One day on my way to piano lessons, I decided to take a shorter route to my grandmother's house, unaware that that would be the day which would change my life forever.

I remember it clearly. I was dressed in garden pants with a beautiful blue blouse and Swedish wooden shoes. My lovely brown hair was swept back in a ponytail. I wanted to get to my grandmother's as fast as possible, being excited as ever about my musical endeavours, and so I took the shorter route through the woods. As it was still daylight I was not concerned about my safety.

Halfway through the the woods near our house, a stranger appeared out of nowhere. A tall slender man in a beige coat. He had short black hair and brown eyes and it did not seem awkward to me to meet a stranger in the woods. He started to talk to me. In Czechoslovakia it wass customary in our upbringing to be told not to go with strangers or accept anything, such as candy from strangers. Moreover, in a socialistic society everything was considered to be reliable, safe and right as rain.

I listened to his story. He told me that he was a policeman. He was investigating the case of two girls who had gone missing. During the search they had recovered the school bags of the girls. But that was the only clue they had. He asked if I could help. Of course, I would! Why wouldn't I? Everybody would help, I thought.

He convinced me of his story. I overlooked the fact that he showed me a dubious photograph to prove his official identity. I believed him, I mean, how could I know what a policeman looked like?

We picked up a conversation and I accompanied him on his way.

'Can I help you carry your bag?' He asked.

I was carrying an open leather bag, and anyone could see its contents.

'Oh yes, thank you' I said, 'I'm going to my grandmother's house for a piano lesson.'

I was like the innocent little-red-riding-hood.

We arrived at some barracks. It looked like a ruin. You could see the ruins of a staircase, parts of a cellar, bits and pieces of the foundation and the fallen rafters of a roof. Some of the walls still stood up straight. At that moment I came to my senses. I realised that I was indeed another little-red-riding-hood – and by my side was a drooling big bad wolf! It felt like lightning had just struck.

What have I been doing?! Why am I walking with a strange man?!

Come on, Iva! You're the smartest of three children, aren't you?

Before I knew it, he pressed his big, rough hand firmly against my mouth. He demanded me to be quiet, to be silent and not scream or go crazy, as he ran his hands all over my child like body. He whispered: 'In a few years your body will become a woman's body'. He lifted me onto a bar and asked me to perform strange motions to his penis with my hand until he was 'ready'.

What is that white goo spurting out of this man, I wondered, this strange man whose gaze hardened into the glittering black eyes of a monstrous wolf? I still could not comprehend where I was and wondered why it was getting so dark and where all the stars had come from.

'Am I already in heaven'? I mysteriously thought to myself.

It was so bright that night considering that in the season darkness came quickly. It seemed that my entire life, brief, but happy up until that point flashed remove by before my eyes. I prayed and felt as if I was going to die.

I thought I would never see my parents, my brother and sister again as I felt half-dead in pain. I started to count to five-hundred since he ordered me to do so. He told me to stay quiet and if I refused to obey, he would kill me. At some point the man got up to go and get something from another room while I stayed quiet on that filthy mattress.

'*Run!*', the thought flashed through my mind. Summoning every bit of bravery, I took to run. I had never run so fast in my entire life. I like to think I was carried by angels all the way across an ugly, stony road in the dark that led out of the forest. Unexpectedly I arrived at a bus stop and at that very moment a bus had stopped. Later I found out that the busses only halted there once every hour and a half!

I felt exhausted and disoriented, I was breathing heavily and I tried to catch my breath while drying the tears in my eyes. I jumped on the bus which was probably sent there by my guardian angels. I still had an appointment to keep with my grandmother. The next day, at daylight, I found out that the 'ugly, stony road' was a tram track! What if a tram had come along and run me over?

'*Why are you so late?*' my grandmother asked me when I arrived. All I could say was that I had been so busy that I had lost track of time. I decided not to tell anybody what I had experienced because I was so ashamed.

I took a deep breath and began to play the piano, but I could not focus and hence I played badly. My grandmother got angry. My hands began to tremble and I felt cold. '*Are you alright?*' she asked but I could not say a single word let alone apologise. I felt so ashamed of my stupidity and naivety.

'*You did not prepare properly for your lesson. You know what will happen next time!*' my grandmother threatened, and she shut the piano with a big bang. My grandfather entered the room, probably attracted by the noise. He too was angry when he learned of my inferior performance. '*You are not prepared for the lesson, so you better come back next time*', he proclaimed.

My eyes fell on the statue of the Dutch milk maid on the piano, which I now see every day. It travelled from the Netherlands to Czechoslovakia and back to the Netherlands again – a piece of mine and my grandmother's history. The gift she received from a Czech uncle that married a Dutch woman in the Netherlands in the early years of the 20th century.

I was so sad and angry at the same time that I disappeared into the dark night towards home. It took me an hour by tram to get home. I returned quiet, cold and I was breathing with a lot of difficulty.

I went straight to bed.

At that time, I did not know anything about what my grandfather had done to my mother. It was much later that I discovered she had been abused by him. By her own father, my dear grandfather who was so nice and loving to everyone. How could this be possible?

Through these experiences my mother could not learn to love herself. She did not want to heal herself even though she was so spiritual, and an inspiration for others. When she finally spoke about her traumatic experience of abuse, no one believed her. This caused her to hate herself even more. We first learnt about it when she turned eighty and my father had already passed away. I wondered if my dad had ever known?

Reflection

My mother did not believe in self-love, but nonetheless she selflessly loved and gave us everything. She did not or could not love herself as she refused to forgive herself, forgive others or forgive the circumstances in which a lot of terrible things had happened to her. She was religious but never attempted to heal her own traumas, especially the trauma of abuse. My own trauma was not healed, maybe because I could not talk about it with my mother. At that time, I did not know my mother had her own secret of abuse at the age of twelve as well. Fortunately, I was able to tell the story to my sister. I was much too ashamed to tell it to my parents. My sister told them, but the story

7. *New York Time bestseller, Louise Hay founded Hay House Publishing Company, started her own spiritual journey after surviving cervical cancer*

was not the full story. Immediately my mother decided to report it to the police.

On the way to the police station we did not talk. I was mortified to talk to my mother about my abuse. My mother did not speak either. It probably reminded her of her own painful experience. Telling my story at the police station was again very raw. A corpulent old police officer was listening to my story without any emotions or empathy at all. In those times girls or women who reported abuse were not taken seriously and certainly not in that temporary Czech culture. Nobody really cared.

Conclusion

I wanted to reveal the dogma of living as a Czech in the communist era, and my experience and that of my family. Those days, the times and my experiences of the reality motivated me to write this book, alongside my transformation inspired by Louise Hay[7] and her book *'You can heal your life'*. Louise Hay states, "Everything follows an unending chain in life, and we know we are everlasting. There is no death of our soul; there is only death of our body." My mother was a soul who went to heaven at the same age as Louise Hay. In the summer of 2017 when she took her last breath, it seemed to signal that it was time for me to get into action and teach the world about self-love through my story.

Hospital 1977 – My Nervus Facialis disorder

A few days after my traumatic experience, I became very ill. At that very moment and being twelve years of age, I had a second audition for a very famous theatre. But I could not, since my illness prevented me to audition. What misfortune. My face had suddenly reddened, and I could barely see out of one eye. It looked like a stroke.

A red rash spread across my entire face as well.

My mother immediately took me to the hospital. It was nothing as innocent as the flu. It was a very dangerous condition called *nervus facialis* disorder. A disorder which could cause permanent facial paralysis. Part of the human face can be even disfigured if not treated early and in the right manner. Thankfully I was admitted to the hospital just in time! The doctors saved my face and eyesight. How could a lady go through life with a disfigured face?

I recovered fully. I had to stay in the hospital for over a month undergoing an antibiotic treatment followed by physical therapy (doing all sorts of facial exercises), chewing gum all the time – my father bought big pieces of gum and chewing gum was a treat in itself. But it was mainly to exercise the muscles in my face. Luckily, I recovered and there was no damage to my face.

My mother visited the hospital with good news: the theatre still wanted to work with me (!) and when I was discharged from the hospital, the theatre asked me to start rehearsing immediately. I will never forget my immense joy.

Reflection

Now I am over fifty, I always look back at my happy past although I live in the present moment. I learn from the past and look forward to discovering more beautiful things in the world. I have realised that we should always reflect on our experiences especially from when we were at the tender age of twelve and thirteen. I was destined to be an artist, a guide, a speaker, an inspirator and I was so convinced I could achieve all that.

Conclusion

The period of social and emotional development in each and everyone's life at the age of twelve to thirteen is known to determine the course of their lives. It is in this period that we strongly feel our purpose and know about our deepest desires. We already feel independent, have a strong opinion of our own, feel a deep sense of responsibility and develop a strong sense of self.

For me, my purpose was crystal clear even while I was struck with disease, while being abused, my purpose was still alive and kicking. The desire to be in front of people, to speak, to perform, to share, to guide, to support, to inspire and to love.

Exercise

Let me assist you with this exercise to find or begin to find your (hidden) purpose. It consists of two steps.

Step 1

The first assignment is the following;

Reflect on the time you were twelve or thirteen years old. Try to find a picture of yourself from this period. Especially a picture of you looking straight at the camera, like a selfie. Take a good close look at it. Keep looking. And let the images and stories come to life. Try to answer the next questions, maybe not all at once. You might want to come back later and add some more that comes to mind. Be patient. It will come.

What comes to your mind first?

....

....

What are the strongest memories you have from that period in your life?

....

....

What is it that you loved doing and you almost could not stop doing?

....

....

What did you love to learn and practice all the time?

....

....

Who were you fond of?

....

....

What experiences made a deep impact (both positive and negative)?

....

....

Where were you (country, surroundings, house, village/town/countryside)?

....

....

What kind of friends did you hang out with?

....

....

What values did you and your friends share? (like for instance, support each other no matter what, always be honest with each other, have fun no matter what, make a difference in other people's lives, doing crazy risky stuff – taking a chance).

....

....

Step 2

Now reflect on your life as a child and focus on your upbringing.

And once again, try to answer some questions;

Do you remember how your parents treated you as a child (loving, strict, liberal, conservative, supportive, religiously et cetera.)? And do you have examples of that?

....

....

Did they try to dictate how you should live, what to look like, what to study or to become, something they did not achieve in their own lives?

....

....

Or did they encourage you in many ways and how did they do that?

....

....

Do you remember a motto filled with standards and values, like a proverb? Something your parents loved to repeat or use as an important lesson in your education? (like for instance; 'only if you work hard, you will achieve success', 'you better choose the right education, so you have the biggest chance to make a good living', 'never look up to nor look down on other people').

....

....

Ok, supposedly you found some answers. Take a good look at it. What do you notice? What is it that strikes you? Do you feel a certain vibe, a strong energy coming up while reading?

Maybe you do not find that purpose or deep desire just yet. However, I guarantee you it will definitely come if you keep reading. And if you have found it already; congratulations! Go for it. Keep at it. Live it.

Church in Czechoslovakia, 1977

After the catastrophe of returning from Egypt, my mother started attending church. It seemed she needed some sort of comfort or some way to keep faith.

Czechoslovakia was and still is one of the countries in Europe housing mostly atheists. The few religious people are mostly Catholics. We as a family became protestant and I was confirmed at the age of fourteen. However, during the communist era, attending church was not permitted. Hence talking about it with others was not really a smart thing to do. I recall one day on our way to church, a friend of mine spotted me and asked me where I was going.

'Oh, just visiting friends.' I replied. I knew she did not believe me.

Communism and Christianity have fundamentally opposing views. In communism you must submit to an ideology and a human leader, in Christianity you should follow the teachings of the Bible and a religious figure. Communism considered itself as the one and only true ideology and finding out that I attended church would have caused problems for me as well as for every member in my family. It would have caused major problems for my mother, she would probably lose her job as a teacher.

Having to attend church in secrecy affected my life negatively; the congregation mainly comprised of the elderly, people who were not disturbed by the authorities. They were of no use to society. It is an indoctrination to keep-them-small-so-they-do-as-they-are-told. People knew society was just like that, and surely there was something wrong about it. But why speak up. Especially when you know you will eventually pay a big price for speaking up.

I wanted to break free and share my journey with others. I wanted to meet people who were also liberating themselves. The possibilities to do so were simply not there.

Let me share a childhood experience of punishment, as it felt like punishment at that time. I must have been thirteen then – quite a difficult age to handle one's emotions and cope with parents emotionally. In that period my father was punished by the communists for his open, and thus conflicting political views, his provocative persona and his tendency to reject popular sentiment.

Back then, I was closest to my mother and hardly knew anything about my father's life. He was like a closed book to me that I was not allowed to read. Years later, after my divorce in the Netherlands, I could draw parallels between my father and my ex-husband. I also realised I did not know my Dutch ex-husband and I had been married to someone I hardly knew. Because he too was emotionally guarded. My father who I got to know in the early years of my childhood in Egypt was entirely different from the man I came to know in the Czech Republic. His career was destroyed, his books banned, and I know that this was what had changed him so drastically.

I recall an incident that showed just how much he had changed. I had sliced some bread earlier and when my father came downstairs to the dining room, he angrily asked:

'Who did this? Who cut the bread from the wrong side? You have to cut the bread from the side that has been sliced already!'

I found his anger about something so trivial amusing and struggled not to laugh. I kept quiet, and smiled. He took one look at me and dashed towards me. I ran but I could not get very far – the kitchen had this tiny room extension where we prepared ingredients for cooking and there I was cornered by him. It all happened very quickly, but it would make the biggest impact on my relationship with my father. He gave me such a slap in my face that it even caused an imprint of his hand on the right side of my young, tender face. I began to cry, shocked and confused about his action. I ran off to my mum to tell her what had happened. I do not recall how it was resolved but I never forgave my father for that appalling act. It was years later, during my transformation I was able to forgive him. Imagine what an impact it was even though such an incident happened only once.

Another example of punishment that I endured was connected to my career. My father wanted me to be an engineer because he had been an engineer. I can now understand why he wanted that. I suppose that the events in 1969 that ended his career were the very reason he was looking for some way of continuing this career through his children. Since my sister was studying medicine and my brother was pursuing his passion, electrical engineering, meant that I – the youngest of the three – was chosen for this purpose. My parents decided that I would be an engineer.

But I wanted to be an actor and singer; I wanted to fully embrace my Bohemian lifestyle. They prohibited that. I also wanted to pursue a career in linguistics, as I was talented in languages. I told them that I wanted to study at the philosophical faculty to learn English and other languages and become an entrepreneur as well as an expert in translation. They refused, especially my father. They argued that there was no success to be found in pursuing such a career and that engineering was a better guaranty for a good career.

This too, for me, was some kind of punishment. At that time, I had no goal, no clear vision, although I had attended a famous theatre as an actress since I was twelve. I deeply and secretly wanted to be on stage and be famous. However something was holding me back and I could not pursue my dreams. Perhaps I feared being punished again.

I remember that my father, fully integrated into a new normal way of life, started offering translation services (how paradoxical!) in several languages including German and English. One day he returned from a trip and we went to pick him up from the station. He took one look at me and said; '*Don't show yourself in front of my eyes, I don't want to see you!*'

He had just heard I did not pass two exams at the university where I studied to be an engineer. In fact, I failed quite dramatically. My self-esteem plummeted and I felt useless. My mother was very kind to me and provided me as much comfort as she could. My father however never again offered any comfort.

Reflection

Through these experiences I recognise the connection between childhood traumas and our relationship with our parents. Most parents are victims themselves of their childhood traumas from which they failed to recover their whole life. Sadly, they create the same traumatic circumstances for their kids, like my father did. It is as if everything is played out in different scenarios and stories but follows the same pattern and the same cycle, over and over again.

I suffered from emotional and physical abuse, which led to an unhealthy focus on being perfect both on the outside and on the inside all the time. I never saw myself as 'good enough', as 'okay', as 'lovable' or even 'likeable'. I lived in the controlling shadow of my father far too long.

I was every bit as entrepreneurial as he was – and still am - but it seemed I was being held back from fulfilling my true potential. I kept seeing myself as 'that little girl' who deserved only punishment and who was always yelled at and told to shut-up and be obedient because that was what was meant to be.

Conclusion

During my years of transformation, I was deeply inspired by Louise Hay and the message of her book *'You can heal your life'*. You can heal your life no matter how old you are. Everything is possible.

The postcard from Prague, 1986

Travelling abroad in those days was hard, if not impossible. It was simply discouraged and a lot of people did not have the resources to do so anyway. 'Stay home in your country, do not go anywhere, you have already arrived in paradise'. That was the motto. Therefore, they made it hard to be able to travel or to even go to Western Europe. It took weeks to get the permit to stay abroad for only a few days.

Fortunately, my mother had an aunt in Switzerland and after she died she left us some money. Because there were no other surviving relatives. Not all of it, because of some unreal regulations we were only allowed to receive a third of the amount.

Still, we could travel envied by a lot of people who did not have those capabilities. People who would therefore spread rumours about us travelling abroad, that we might be doing things that could threaten our beloved country. My mother, being a wise and smart woman, kept quiet and she kept quiet about a lot of other things, being afraid to face some weird or unthinkable consequence. Forever protecting herself and her family.

The following is a story involving my time at the university and the ridiculous priorities we were subjected to in communist Czechoslovakia. How it felt to be trapped in an educational program you would never want to follow. It is an experience I would never forget.

In the summer of 1986 we were at the border and the customs officers practically turned our whole car upside down. My father was stripped, they searched for something under the car using mirrors on a stick, we had to declare what we had, they checked if we attempted to carry any foreign currencies. After all that fuss, we finally arrived in Spain for a short holiday. I was twenty-one years old. We were finally enjoying our vacation.

After our return, one early morning, I woke up, prepared myself and left as usual to attend lectures at the technical university. I stepped into a very high building and was told that the political teacher wanted to see me. Politics was a very important issue and an integral subject of all our studies because of Communism. So, you can understand the sphere of influence this particular teacher had. When I got into his office, the first thing I spotted was a statue of Lenin on his desk. The teacher looked at me with strange emotionless eyes and asked, *'What did you do?'*

I looked back in surprise. *'What do you mean, comrade?'* Back then everyone was called 'comrade'. He showed me a postcard – a postcard sent from Prague. The postcard expressed how much I disagreed with his political views as well as the communist philosophy. It had been signed by 'me', apparently. I looked up from the postcard and told him it was impossible for me to have sent the postcard. I was abroad at the time, in Spain to be precise. It was summer, and I was abroad for the first few weeks of my holiday, therefore it was impossible for me to have sent a postcard from Czechoslovakia. Surely, he was accusing me of sending some political motivated texts within Czechoslovakia.

He replied, *'Then who could it be since it is your name on the postcard?'*

I answered, *'It's not my signature. My signature and handwriting are totally different from what is written on the postcard. Please have a look.'*

I demonstrated by writing some lines of texts on a piece of paper.

He still did not believe me as suspicious as he was. I remember feeling like a political criminal and at that time I realised the possibility that I may not pass my second tier of study because of the political nature in this situation. I was feeling totally trapped and cornered, he said to me; *'Ok, you now have only one chance to prove yourself. You will learn everything by heart from Marx, Engels and Lenin[8] . If you don't, I will not admit you to write any political exams and you will not succeed the second tier of your study'.*

---

8. *Marxism-Leninism was the political ideology adopted by the Communist Party of the Soviet Union. Czechoslovakia was then part of the socialist states or eastern bloc.*

He continued, raising the volume of his voice; *'That's it, now go, go! And shut the door behind you on your way out. I don't want to see you anymore. Get out of my sight!'*

What particularly confused me a few months later is that I got a silver medal (it was an honour) in a national competition of all universities on the political presentation of dialectic, materialistic conception of beauty. How could I have managed to represent my faculty on such a topic? Not being myself, not aware of what I was doing, I felt lost. The dogma was so deep, and the fear was so strong that I did not realise I was sinking into the very thing I despised and stood up against. The feeling of being numbed and confined.

I left the room. As I walked through the corridor, I wept. I wept because I was wondering who was so jealous of me. Who could do such a thing! Could it possibly have anything to do with my trips abroad? It occurred to me why my mother lived with so much caution – she constantly talked about the importance of not telling people about our business or holiday travels. We had created the possibility to travel and I could not understand how someone could be so jealous of that to go so far to want to destroy my future career. Why? What was the reason? Who was this person? I still do not know who tried to frame me back then.

A week later I went back to see the political teacher with his strange cruel eyes, and the big statue of Lenin on his desk, which I will never forget. I had memorised all literature that was expected of me. While reciting the definitions, I realised I had forgotten one word from studying the literature. I panicked, I almost freaked out and my voice dried up in my throat. I knew the rest of my definitions were okay, but I had forgotten one line from Marx. Oh my God!

The man responded;

'Ok, you have to go back and memorise everything and then return because you do not know it. You must think! For heaven's sake, use your brain!' he added.

While standing there I suddenly realised that he had just given me a clue – I missed the definition about thinking. I looked at his desk with the imposing statue of Lenin on it, turned around and quickly slipped out of his room.

When I came before him a week later I thought I would miss my opportunity again. But I did not. At the end of my recitation he expressed his satisfaction. Still he maintained he would never forget what I had written on that very postcard. Eventually I was admitted to writing the political exam.

Reflection

This man was behaving out of fear. To live in fear was at that time for most people the only option. Nowadays I still see most people who live in fear, being unconscious of what they are choosing and doing, people who are pursuing a career or going in a direction that is not suited to them and that might actually destroy them – they look outside trying to live up to society's expectations instead of looking inside to who they truly are and who they want to be. In those times it was even more reinforced. You had to survive, so everything people did was focused on that very survival. And solely that. Day by day.

Conclusion

Truth is outplayed in an atmosphere of oppression. It is highly unwelcome. It is even threatening to those who play the game of oppression. Truth lying deep inside each one of us is like an unknown place. It can only be known if we open ourselves up to it. It's like shifting a paradigm. From being oppressed or put down to being liberated. It seems frightening, but it is so near. It's inside you already. Not out there, inside! Take a close look. You will find it, I'm sure.

First Job in Czechoslovakia, 1989

Starting a career in an international company was meant to be only for a few at the time. There were only a few companies during the communist era that could do business with western countries. Still, I succeeded in finding a respectable job at an international trade company and found myself in the capital of Slovakia, Bratislava. Usually only lucky communists could work there at that time. I realised that this was the life I wanted to live at that moment. I had my first contracts and travelled quite a lot. My sister was living in West Germany, so I could visit her more often.

It was not easy to travel to western countries in those days. You could not travel to Western Europe for business purposes, scared as they were that critical intellectual or political information would leave the country and that would possibly be harmful for the regime. I found it all so contradictory because in my private life I could travel to the west to visit my sister without any restrictions.

At the time my conscious mind was focused only on work-work-work and making money. I had no time to be distracted by such confusing practices.

Prague and abortion, 1991

I took a job in Prague because my Dutch boyfriend wanted to move to Prague to start his own business there, a restaurant. We met in 1990 in Czechoslovakia and one year later he decided to move to Prague. I left the company in Bratislava, my fantastic career job to find my new happiness in Prague, finding a new job, a new apartment for us and arranging all other necessities. This all in two months time. When he came, everything was arranged. I never got a thank you. I never argued. I was in love. I saw that my job selection was based on how much salary I could earn, not on my experience or occupation.

I got pregnant. I did not know what to do, feeling desperate, because there was no support from my boyfriend. He wanted me to have an abortion. It was very painful for me. At that time, it felt like a huge burden to me. To feel the responsibility of life or death of something so precious and vulnerable. It felt like a major mistake. I kept these thoughts to myself and we never talked about it again.

I remember the day we took the bus from Prague for a weekend to see my parents in Brno (the city where I also grew up). It was just an ordinary day and we again did not talk about it. There was only a deadly silence. I was very sad and at the same time I was not aware of what I was doing to my body at all.

When we arrived at Brno we met the gynaecologist at the hospital. She was a friend of my sister and she looked firmly at my boyfriend. Out of the blue, she discretely said to me; '*It seems you two are not fit for each other*'. It is funny and yet so tragic considering that two years later, shortly after we moved to the Netherlands, I married him and I got pregnant again. However, after thirteen years of marriage I divorced him. The friend from hospital proved to be right. The next chapter in my life had started; being a single mum living abroad.

Chapter III

Emigration to the Netherlands, 1992 after the velvet revolution in Czechoslovakia

'Yesterday I was clever, so I wanted to change the world.
Today I'm wise, so I'm changing myself.'

- Mowlana Jalaluddin Rumi [9]

When I first came to the Netherlands, everything felt like a fairy tale. Well, not entirely like a fairy tale but when I intuitively jumped into the car for the one-way journey from Prague to the Netherlands, I believed everything would be fine.

My first year, however, was a struggle. A struggle with myself. Not knowing who I was. It was also a struggle to find my first job. It wasn't easy for a Czech woman with a technical background to find a similar position at the same level of seniority in the Netherlands. I still had to learn the language to begin with.

I first started helping the elderly and started cleaning houses for a care, service and cleaning company. It was a rewarding experience because people were happy with me, especially because the manager knew my professional background. She only gave me jobs to do in which I did not have to do the real dirty jobs like cleaning toilets. One

---

9. *Mowlana Jalaluddin Rumi was a 13th-century Persian poet and theologian. His poems and spiritual legacy have been widely translated into many of the world's languages.*

time I remember I was assigned to handle the kids of a stressed out single father who had no one to take care of them; another time I took care of a lonely alcoholic woman; and yet another time, I handled a sick, financially broke woman who was living with five rabbits in her living room.

These encounters formed a part of my initial experience with the Dutch. Sometimes I wondered: I know there is nothing worse than the communist society I grew up in but what is going on here? For instance; you had to make an appointment whenever you wanted to meet anyone or make something happen. People perceived me as someone from another planet, feeling lost like some outsider or even worse, an 'alien', even though I spoke the language fluently within three months.

Within ten months, I was glad to find my first professional job. My husband still could neither support me nor himself, not financially let alone emotionally as he was forever 'studying' – trapped in the rut of a half-finished degree. This increased the pressure on me to support the both of us. In the meantime, I held on to my naive belief that he would change one day, and things would eventually get much better. Since it overwhelmed me to face so many contrasts and challenges, I often found myself sitting in my car, crying.

In my new job, there were colleagues who did not respect me at all. One day there was a client who bought some chemicals. He literally said he would like to spray all the foreigners living in the Netherlands if he could.

Don't get me wrong, I am positive about the Dutch but at that time there were a lot of people hating on foreigners. I was a magnet for them. More so because I did not love myself. Now I know I did not respect myself either and I did not know better at that time. It was to be expected in the early 90's as there was a totally different approach to how foreigners were seen and treated. Foreigners were seen and treated as intruders, like they were humans of lesser quality and ability. Of course, the European Union did not exist back then, so I had to go and register myself at the police station (no immigration office in those days) for some work and residence permit each year. I remember feeling like a criminal every time I went there.

From my salary, I was able to buy our first apartment and get a mortgage. As my father contributed too, I was able to do this through some financially sound decision making. The belief, our parents gave us in our upbringing is that it is important to be financially secure and they supported me in making those decisions.

It was quite a strange, sobering experience for me when we bought the apartment. I had grown up in a beautiful, big house in Brno which my father had built himself. It came with a sprawling view and a lovely environment. But here I was, buying a tiny (8 by 10 metres), ugly apartment to live in for the both of us. My sister refused to keep her mouth shut when she saw the apartment. She clearly showed her dislike. I, however, was happy and satisfied at that moment.

We got married in the Dominican Republic. We had a nice ceremony combined with a church wedding in the Netherlands. Marrying in a church was not something my boyfriend liked but I persuaded him to do so for the sake of family and friends. Already by then, it seemed as if I continuously had to struggle to persuade him let alone have some sort of influence on him or his behaviour. I tried to convince him to finish his studies, but he refused to do so. Something he regretted later in life. At that time I did not realise that I was the one that needed to change to be able to change others. I tried so hard to change him without any success. It is not until we realise that we need to change first before we can change others, we won't be able to affect anybody at all.

When our first daughter was born, I was happy, yes, ecstatic even, because I had already been through an unwanted abortion before. Watching my daughter grow up, learn ballet, and to play the piano was a period of absolute joy.

I often thought I was lost in a society without emotions. People were quite often exchanging only the superficial stuff, being afraid to share emotions or show the true expressions of the soul. People are internally quite often broken. I've seen and spoken to so many couples that were keeping up appearances and yet were blaming one another for a lot.

We moved to a newly built house. That's where my destructive thinking started all over again. I started having lots of challenges at work. I remember starting a job in the aerospace industry where I changed my career into procurement and started studying again at the age of thirty-six. The workplace was filled with sexism and bullying; I was too scared to complain or do something about it for the fear of losing my job. So, I kept quiet about it.

It was a place dominated by males who expressed their masculinity openly. One day a colleague waited for me in the parking lot and grabbed me with his big hands. I struggled to escape, screaming that he was crazy, but he held on to me and said *'stop resisting, you only live once!'* Another time, another colleague waited very conspicuously for me in the elevator and had been very clear about his ill intentions. It all frightened me a lot. All this time I had heard how tolerant the Dutch were and how open minded they were. But in my experience, I was neither tolerated nor respected.

After 9/11, the company closed. Maybe it was a sign that I should have chosen to be self-employed just before the company broke down. In those days it was so hard to get a new job. In 2002, I was faced with new challenges again. Every year comes with its own challenges, yet this year seemed different.

First of all, I had no job — the company was liquidated. I did not realise it would be so difficult to find another job. The choice I made at that time to not accept a temporary contract paved my future. Secondly, I had a miscarriage on the 18th of June, my birthday. How about that!? In the hospital they could not find a heartbeat and I was presented with the fact that my baby was dead. I ended up crying in the parking lot where everybody could see me. My seven-year-old daughter was with me that day. I remember looking in her face for just a moment. I could clearly notice that it was a shocking experience for her to see me cry. She did not know what to do.

On the 23rd of October 2002, my father passed away. I knew there was something different about him when I flew to visit him a few days before his death. Somehow, I knew my father wanted to see me once more as if he knew this would be the last chance to see me before he would die. He had been ill and fighting against diabetes for so long, but there were no indications of any kind that he would pass away soon. Two days after my arrival, my visit to him was one of great sadness, the weather, stormy and horrible, seemed to agree with the sentiments in my dad's hospital room. I held his hand as he did not say anything. I showed him pictures of my daughter and offered him some rice to eat. He did not respond to any of it. He was probably too tired and too weak to do anything.

I turned to my brother; '*This doesn't look good. Something is going on,*' I said. '*They do not give him insulin anymore. What's going on?*'

I was confused. We decided to go back the next day to keep an eye on him. My father was awake and feeling a little better. He wanted some herring, his favourite fish. I hurried to the supermarket to buy some which pleased him very much. There was a moment of connection. I could feel and sense it. That evening, my mother took me to the theatre; "One flew over the cuckoo's nest" was on, based on a famous movie. It was an evening for us to reflect on my father's life, his struggles and depression right after he had lost everything. Somehow this reflecting and reminiscing had some healing power for the both of us.

The next morning, the telephone rang. My mother picked up the phone and after many moments that passed in silence, she started to cry. I asked her what was wrong. She said: '*Ivanka... Dad has passed away*'. And that he was already in mortuary. Shocked by this sudden news, we jumped into the car and sped to hospital. It was of course too late.

We were more than astonished. No matter in what country you

live, it is indescribably inhumane to prevent a family from seeing a loved one who had just passed away. No one of the hospital staff was willing to speak to us, so I asked a patient in the ward if he knew anything about what had happened. He could tell me that my father started experiencing severe pains during the night and that no one came to help him. He was lying there in pain, with no medication or any medical help. By 7:00 am he died. We were informed by 10:00 am. In those three hours they had cleaned him up and taken him to mortuary. No one bothered to inform us. I simply could not understand.

I screamed at the doctors that I had to see my father, but they said it wasn't possible. Whatever I tried I was not allowed to see my father anymore. Right there it struck me. It felt like I was living in the communist regime again. And my mother? My mother brought a bottle of whiskey to thank the doctor in exchange for his services. I could not believe what I saw and screamed at her; *'What kind of service? Are you crazy? What kind of service?'* I still can't believe what had happened that very morning.

After I made all the arrangements for the funeral together with my mother I had to return to the Netherlands because I had to take two exams. I was studying procurement management at the time. Everyone thought I had gone crazy because I took off just before the funeral would take place. I left my mother all by herself. But I passed the exams and immediately rushed back to Prague, conquering another 1200 km. After the funeral we went back again to the Netherlands. Now I realise how crazy I must have been. I even left my mother the day after the funeral because I had a crucial job interview. I desperately needed a job. So, I set off with my daughter and husband to drive yet another 1200 km.

When my second daughter was born, in 2004, there was only one year of celebrating our newly born daughter together. In 2006 when my first daughter was thirteen and the youngest daughter two, my marriage collapsed. By 2007, we were officially divorced and my Dutch husband left me all by myself with my two girls and disappeared; never to return. Not a sign of life since then. He seemed to have vanished into thin air.

I had to handle everything myself. A single mum in a foreign country. I handled everything without support from my family – my sister was in Germany, which seemed like the other end of the world and my brother was even further away in the Czech Republic. No one offered any kind of assistance as they all viewed me as a strong independent woman.

Why did nobody offer any help? Right! I did not ask for it. Why? Because I was not aware and simply followed the footsteps of my mother living the motto; "I will do everything on my own, nobody needs to help me". And so, I did. I was not conscious of the fact that not asking for help blocked me from my own happiness.

From repairing the lights, to cleaning the windows in the middle of the night or baking cookies after midnight; I did it all by myself. Indeed, I looked very strong from the outside, but I was broken on the inside. I think the divorce had a strong impact on how my career progressed from that point and why it took so much time to change myself. I did not see the real Iva, I had turned into a Zombie-Iva, acting and living someone else's life.

I held on to this erroneous belief, although, the universe was repeatedly telling me to change!

Yes, I was like a 'monkey' who had to be fired, bullied and not respected at all before I recognised that I had to change something. In other words, I deserved a lot of ass kicking before I started to move and change things.

Sometimes when I arrived at work, my colleagues would ask *'Hey Iva, what's that you've got on your jacket?'* They would probably be referring to dried burp or food stains. 'Attractive' left-overs from taking care of my baby when feeding her in the early mornings. The journey to and from work was over 50 km. I would return home to cook in the evening and then clean the house until 1: 00 am before going to sleep. I dragged myself from one day to the next. Feeling numbed, docile and with no sense of direction or purpose.

I started dating again around that time – but again, with the wrong man. I was still pursuing something outside myself to find fulfilment. I had not found 'me' yet. I was balancing with everything, trying to make everybody happy but myself.

Who was 'me'?

I was cut off from my family and my identity.

Who was 'me'?

Was I Czech, Egyptian or Dutch?

I was born in Egypt and I grew up in Czechoslovakia. After my studies and move to the Netherlands I did not know where my life was heading. I was not conscious of the path my life was taking. All my father wanted was to escape communism, my mother did not; and I, after migrating from the Czech Republic to the Netherlands just wanted to escape the tragedy that befell a lot of Czechs. I had a Czech boyfriend back then, but I knew that I never wanted to settle down with him. This was caused by the tragedy of my parent's marriage. I hated the country and I hated the communists because of the circumstances they had put us in.

When I was a little child, I often saw my mother cry. I remember the day that, in total annoyance, she smashed a fist through the window breaking it. The true meaning of her frustration was unknown to me. I could only guess that she was a devastated woman because of how much communism had taken from us. My father lost everything because of his provocative and anti-communist views. He was punished unfairly for his individual mind-set. I felt punished unfairly too when my mother passed away, leaving me behind as an orphan.

Sometimes I think deeply about the tragic circumstances that drove us out of Egypt. Why did my father lose everything? Why did my mother not want to talk about it? Why could we talk about everything else in my family but never about those events? In my family we expressed ourselves very well but because of the fear for the truth my parents never spoke about those tragic events. It was just too painful.

Self-development of Emotional Intelligence

It was an ordinary autumn day. Almost all leaves had fallen on the ground and I was driving to work; my real full-time job was feeding my kids and building a future for them. I wasn't focused on my future or my own happiness. I lived in survival mode.

That morning, I had a very strange feeling – a strange feeling about the activities in my company. I could not identify these hunches. I got to work and there was someone from human resources next to my office. She was never there because her office was at the other side of town. I came in, powered up my laptop, checked my phone and started the day. I opened my email and responded to pending mails.

Somehow, I was very nervous and did not understand why. I was so nervous that I could not concentrate. It was almost like I was going to have some emotional breakdown. Right at that moment one of my colleagues dropped by, a fellow who had been a constant bully in the past. He said; *'I couldn't sleep at all last night, I had such bad dreams'*. I did not think much about it but in a few hours, I would understand exactly what he meant.

This was the very same guy who liked to nickname me 'Diva'. For no reason at all. Asking me very often and provocatively why I did not wear short skirts and asking me again and again what my private life was like. One day I thought let's make a practical joke with him. Let's see what happens. I bought a big box of chocolates branded with the actual brand name 'Diva' and put them openly on my desk. You should have seen his face. It was hilarious.

This man had gone to my boss, the technical director, several times behind my back to complain about me. The man accused me of trying to destroy the organisation they had built. He claimed I was arrogant, that I was looking down on other people. He also accused me that I was single-handedly trying to change all sorts of things within the company. Trying to get things done my way. He falsely accused me of so many things. When I was summoned by my boss, I learnt about these accusations and I stared at him in total surprise.

My boss yelled and screamed in anger. He asked, *"who the hell do you think you are?"*, questioning his leadership. He then asked if I had succeeded in solving an issue that had happened a while ago. I was asked to address a procurement issue with a supplier which had occurred prior to me joining the company. I did try to fix it; I asked for more information and hand-outs that would better help me understand the situation. I did my due diligence thoroughly in my attempt to solve the situation.

The goods were neglected in storage for half a year and it seemed that the whole matter had been abandoned by management themselves. Suddenly it had become a big problem. A problem, would you believe, I had failed to handle. Not the fault of my boss – who was always right – but it was my fault. I made the mistake.

Funny enough we had this sign leading to the toilets – men to the left and women to the right. I knew I was right this time but here he was entering the ladies.

This all happened before I started my transformational journey and I did not realise then that he was the one with the problem. He was behaving like a little child throwing a tantrum over a toy he did not get. Looking back, it all seems very funny and amusing. There are so many people out there who behave in a similar fashion, who do not know why they behave the way they do. It is hilarious and funny from afar, it is deeply tragic when you are confronted with it.

For a second time that day, I was summoned, but not by him, rather the lady from human resources. A few hours after being bullied by my boss. She quietly entered my office and asked if I could join her at the board of directors' office. At that moment I immediately knew what was going on. I could sense what was coming.

In that very instant I recalled an event that a manager who was popular among all his colleagues suddenly got fired that previous month. He had a huge fight with the technical director and he was punished with his dismissal after having worked for twenty years for the company. No one knew why he was fired. He warned me several times to be careful. When we occasionally met for lunch or talked to each other at the coffee machine we were both unaware of the politics that was going on. Let alone what was going to come. We both did not know it would be the end of both our jobs. Several weeks later it all became crystal clear.

One day all employees were asked to go to the staff restaurant where we were informed about his dismissal. I was in shock. How could the boss assemble all the employees for such an announcement? Were they trying to set an example? Were they trying to scare everyone? And from then on, I thought, *'did I choose the right company?'*, *'would I be happy to conform to everything in order to survive?'*

I concluded that it meant that I too had 'to eat other rats[10] to survive', if you know what I mean. Or else, who would win this rat race? Was I going to survive or let other people eat my cheese? I did not fall for that rat trap, I am not a rat; In fact, I am a snake in Chinese astrology. Snakes are usually contemplating, intuitive, mysterious, wise and only strike when they are in real danger.

When I entered the board of directors' office, to my surprise my boss was there also, and he asked me to sit down. My emotions were in an upheaval. I did not know what was going on. He had pieces of paper lying in front of him as if he wanted to hand them over. The human resources woman was sitting next to him. I sat down, looking straight at them. They could not look back. They did not want to face the reality of the situation considering that they were scared to be unmasked. My boss said to me; *'You can go home right now. Leave your laptop and mobile phone right here. Don't talk to anyone, do not try to finish something you started'*.

I was just in the middle of the preparation of a contract and I had several meetings lined up for the day. Everything was terminated. Right there and then.

10. *The Way of the Rat: A survival guide to office politics Paperback – 2004 – by Joep P.M. Schrijvers*

I could not breathe. I was silent for a while. I was speechless. It felt like I could just die in that moment. Memories arose, memories of the times when I was unemployed as I came to the Netherlands trying to find a job and make a living. I had been in a company that went bankrupt and had been bullied in many companies before. But this was smoother, subtler; I did my job well; lots of colleagues liked me. However, some did not as expected, and they had slowly dug a grave for me.

This was the point I understood what the guy meant earlier that morning. The guy who had slandered me to the boss. Several directors had ignored me since I arrived and I realised why I had not received any response to the emails I had sent earlier.

People can behave like little children, living without any consciousness; but just as satisfied with their 9 to 5 job, protecting those jobs with whatever they have. Most people just want to be like others, because when you step out from the crowd you create problems. It is very much the story of the corporate world and in general, society as a whole. We must fit within social norms. Following the flock. Not knowing our 'why', why and how the company can be fruitful and its intrinsic motivation.

That day was a catastrophe. The drizzle that began earlier that morning had become a heavy downpour. I received a letter in which they asked me to sign my acceptance of resignation and that I would receive one month's salary. I was told I could get a lawyer. I told them I needed a while to read the letter and that I could not sign it without doing so. They allowed me an hour. I felt like I was locked in a pressure cooker and I could not escape. Desperately feeling cross as a frog in a sock. I could not read at all. I just kept saying to myself; *'Iva keep silent, don't do anything rash!'*.

The other colleagues I had helped to organise the department of procurement were called in as well, but they were kept in a separate room, so they could not talk with me. Probably they were informed about my dismissal.

I felt humiliated and put down. I had no time to say goodbye or pack my things. I wanted to say goodbye to so many people. However, I did not get the chance thus leaving a blank space for anyone with an imagination to fill in regarding the reason on why I had to leave. I got an hour to do so in my office. After twenty minutes the human resources woman came in for a second time while I was sorting through my stuff and she asked me, no she urged me to hurry up and leave.

Whatever they used as the reason for my resignation I still do not know. I just did not care, anymore. I was happy I was able to leave with my personal belongings. When I started this job, they wanted me to have one phone, but I insisted on keeping my personal and business phones separate. I was glad I had made that decision. As I left the building and went to my car, I felt nauseous. I sat down in my car; I could not breath and I started to cry. Somehow, I managed to start the car and drive. The feelings were so intense that I had to pull up at the nearest parking spot. I called a friend and asked if I could visit her to talk. She said I could. *'Can you drive?'* *'Sure, yes I can'* I replied with some sort of resilience. I drove down to see her, and she was very comforting and supportive.

After some while I regained my common senses and I decided I had to stand up for myself. When the legal proceedings started I had chosen a good lawyer. This lawyer was well trained, and he did an excellent job handling my case. At first when he saw the letter, he started to laugh. He asked me to entrust the letter to him and that he would handle the case. And so, he did. First, he requested the reasons for my dismissal from the organisation.

Their reasons were ridiculous: that I was not helping in the restaurant, in the kitchen or taking stuff out of the washing machine. That I was arrogant and not cooperative. That I was not a team player, not willing and not being supportive to my colleagues.

The lawyer was of immense help. He laid down several options for me. I had the option to go for a trial or to take the amount my company had offered. He said the possibility was that I would win the case. He explained that the way I had been dismissed was unlawful. And yes, we won the case.

I realised that this is a problem occurring in our society – that people use their so-called strength to hurt others. They do not see human souls, just numbers. This has helped me a lot to realise that I am more than just a number, rather a human being with the responsibility to live a meaningful life by helping others. The people that tried to get me down could be clients that I could help, to be happy again. That I can help them by solving the many childhood issues and trauma they must have suffered in the past. I pray for them. I forgive them.

Reflection

When I look back at the first fifty years of my life, I would say that the first fifty years of each life are the most difficult and complicated ones. The first fifty years were something like an extended childhood to me. Life however starts at fifty. It is an age for a new beginning. With that age comes the urge to fully embrace oneself as a complete individual. Self-love becomes apparent and obvious. Sharing of it and inspiring others also. It is possible for everyone to be okay with themselves, so everybody will be okay. This is not some Utopian message. It is seeded in all of us, right from the start. Joy, love, resilience, well-being, peace, they are all innate. Just rediscover and nurture them, each day.

The Laws of Human Suffering

'People have a tough time letting go of their suffering. Out of a fear of the unknown, they prefer suffering that's familiar.'

-Thich Nhat Hanh[11]

Thinking about my experiences as I have shared in this chapter, three truths stand out clearly to me which I believe are universally true:

1. We and the ones we love will often go through suffering and misery that is beyond our control.

    I could not help my failing father before he died; his pain and misery over the years were something beyond his control. But still the pain and suffering we cannot control teaches us acceptance. In the end, it doesn't matter what happens to us, but what happens inside of us. When our pain can no longer sting and make us bitter it will make us more beautiful instead. Like a crushed rose that still releases a nice fragrance. We truly transform.

2. There will always be those who will seek to exploit our suffering and pain to push their own plan, to promote themselves, or get us to focus on them. It's our challenge to see through that and be compassionate towards them.

    When people try to use pain and suffering against us, our greatest victory is not in being able to fight back but in the love and forgiveness that is awakened in our hearts towards

---

11. *Zen Master Thich Nhat Hanh is a global spiritual leader, poet and peace activist, revered around the world for his powerful teachings and bestselling writings on mindfulness and peace. His best-known book is "Peace is every step".*

them. Nothing disarms an enemy more than goodwill in return. Despite being treated so badly, I was able to see through the terrible behaviour of my seniors in that company where I was sacked to realise that they were victims of soul injuries they may have suffered in their childhood.

3. There is always something we can do to help reduce another's pain and misery.

We always have the power to do good. Being in control of our will means we can always be in the position to do good. Moreover, we are born with innate joy, peace, well-being and resilience. That goodness serves others and ourselves. It is that innateness that can create deep connections between people. Good people standing by while others are punished unjustly all points to a huge flaw in society. It teaches us there is a great necessity to know that we are innately alright, all of us.

I am blessed to have found these laws because they were the bases of my life after fifty.

MY NEW LIFE

Chapter IV

Knowing who I am and what I want

'The person I'm seeking is also seeking me - we are being brought together on the checker board of life.'

- Louise Hay[12]

As you travel through life;

As you travel through life;
There are always those times
When decisions just have to be made,
When the choices are hard,
And solutions seem scarce;
And the rain seems
To soak your parade!

There are some situations
Where all you can do
Is to simply let go and move on.

12. Louise Hay was speaker, healer, artist and author of amongst others the book "You can heal your life"

Gather courage together
And choose a direction
That carries you toward a new dawn.

So, pack up your troubles
And take a step forward;
The process of change can be tough,
But think about all the excitement ahead;
If you can be stalwart enough!

There could be adventures
You never imagined
Just waiting around the next bend.
And wishes and dreams
Just 'bout to come true
In ways you can't yet comprehend!

Perhaps you'll find friendships,
That spring from new interests,
As you challenge your status quo
And learn there are so many
Options in life;
And so many ways you can grow!

Perhaps you'll go places
You never expected
And see things that you've never seen
Or travel to fabulous,
Faraway worlds

And wonderful spots in between!

Perhaps you'll find warmth
And affection and caring,
A "somebody special" who's there
To help you stay centred
And listen with interest
To stories and feelings, you share.

Perhaps you'll find comfort
In knowing your friends are
Supportive of all that you do
And believe that whatever
Decisions you make,
They'll be the right choices for you!

So, keep putting one foot
In front of the other
And taking your life
Day by day.

There's a brighter tomorrow
That's just down the road.
Don't look back.
You're not going that way!

(author unknown)

The day I started to change my old habbits

A day becomes a week; a week becomes a month; a month becomes a year. The years become our destiny. And everything stays the same over and over again.

-Iva Schubart

When you are at the end of the year and have some resolutions for the New Year and do not write anything down, nothing will happen. We are supposed to do something new each year. Therefore, many of us make resolutions such as to start a diet, or to try to accomplish anything that is meaningful.

However, by the end of January or maybe some months later, we have stopped with our diet or our fitness plan. We have abandoned it quicker than an old toy being replaced by a new one when it arrives. While we think we are consciously making decisions to change, our inner voice is saying something totally different – meaning our subconscious mind is in control. There are many teachings about how you can transform yourself by taking control of your subconscious mind. Among them are the teachings of Thich Nhat Hanh which I highly recommend.

What screws us up most in life is the picture we have in our head of how our reality is supposed to be. My view of reality was distorted as well. When I first decided to study quantum physics and the law of attraction in the USA, my point of view started to shift. Reading and teaching was one thing, application of it in daily life was another – it was much more difficult than I thought. It is like we understand what skiing is and think we can start skiing very well immediately. Owning skis and having read everything there is to know about skiing is not the same as knowing how to ski – it requires exercise. A lot of it, if you want to get really skilled at it.

When we have a goal and we want to make it happen we must act. An action in the direction to where we want to be. Was it easy to me? Is it easy for you? Of course not. Without courage and effort, you cannot reach your dreams. Constant and consistent action will move you in the direction you want to go.

My past carved some very deep wounds in my soul - communism, rape, hospitalized to the verge of a near death experience at the age of three facing Dengue fever, the mental disclosure and depression of my father after he lost his career in 1970 and also caused by putting his signature on Charter 1977 - a declaration of a movement run by intellectuals and artists who fought for fundamental human rights - and last but not least, the sudden emigration to the Netherlands, bullying, initial discrimination in the Netherlands, my divorce, my abortion to name a few.

Despite these deep wounds I still had a deep desire to heal. My path was covered with obstacles and dark moments. My energy in my mind, body and soul was very low. One day, I started to talk to my mother about my journey. She knew I would find the greatest version of myself and she often called me the sunshine and the love and light of the family. *'Your spiritual development is amazing'*, she told me once when I was still fighting with my divorce.

Since you are reading my book, you too must be searching for a better and meaningful life even though you might have gone through different and difficult challenges as I had. When you want to increase the quality of your life you have to leave everything behind which does not serve a purpose in your life anymore - people, stuff, places, symbols and especially habits that causes you nothing but grief and pain.

Like I did. I left all those stories behind me. I will show you how to do so as well and help you to leave yours behind. It will show you how amazingly resilient and powerful you are. So, let's start.

Three questions to start with;

- Are you ready to replace everything that does not serve you anymore?
- Are you willing to start new habits and write them down?
- Are you committed to start doing it and never give in, to be the person you want to be?

Write your new habits down, at least 5 of them:

1.

2.

3.

4.

5.

When you start to build new habits (for instance start exercising each morning for about thirty minutes or eat breakfast without any kind of distractions such as your smartphone, the internet or television or write down what you are grateful for each day), you gain a new skill with which your inner power begins to grow. When you stick to these habits for at least forty days, you start to transform. The journey of transformation is not easy but well worth it.

Adding to your transformation, know that there are 5 truths to regain power over your life again and to be able to make a lasting change in your life;

- You are already a complete person with nothing missing. God or the universe, or whatever its name, made us complete and whole already.
- You are a creative being. Our nature is to always be creating, good or bad.
- You create from your beliefs about yourself.

- You have made conscious decisions about yourself, others and life; decisions which are now unconscious, and this unconscious mindset influences your decisions and ultimately determine the quality of your life.

The universe is cooperative and supportive. It says yes to both the good and bad ideas, even if the ideas will destroy you.

The power of thoughts creates who we are, and our destructive thinking makes us small in business as well as our personal lives. When we start to pay attention to our thoughts and how our thoughts influence our feelings and start to investigate them, a shift starts to happen.

This was what happened to me. Sitting in my living room and reflecting on my thoughts and my tumultuous emotions, I realised I was destroying myself and hurting myself in the process – entirely myself. The light dawned on me and my habits and thoughts started to shift. And I transformed.

'The biggest wakeup call you can ever get is to actually live the life you love'

- Iva Schubart

Tough truths

Do you examine tough truths about your life? I examined such truths when I started my transformation. I remember the time when my mother died in the summer of 2017; it is still fresh in my mind and the pain is indescribable. She was far away from me in Czech republic and I wanted to be with her in her last moments of life, but I could not do anything. When I heard the news of her death, it took me no time to fly to Vienna and travel another hour to Brno, the Czech Republic only to realise that I was never be able to hold her again. She had already been moved to the local morgue. I could not even embrace her one more time. That was a cold hard fact to swallow and to cope with.

She was stored in a cold chamber in the morgue and I was not allowed to see her anymore. No exceptions, not even for a family member who had to travel from far. It was like history repeating itself. When my father died the same happened. That made this truth even harder to deal with.

Imagine

So, imagine you are at the end of your life and you are not going to meet tomorrow. Imagine that all the people you care about and all the people that love you are gone, as are your friends. From that point of view, look back at your 'past' and think of the things you would have changed or would have done differently. These are your 'tough truths'.

Let's start with the following questions;

How do you feel about your life thus far?

Do you have any regrets?

Marshall Goldsmith[13] carried out a research in which he interviewed a group of successful leaders and another group of 'regular' people at the end of their lives. They used the same questions for both groups to find out what they truly valued in life. Remarkable enough, the answers were similar. It seems that the four valuable things I am about to present are true for anybody on our planet.

Ranked by importance;

First: Pleasure, happiness

Second: Relationships

13. *World-renowned business educator and coach, Dr. Marshall Goldsmith is the leading expert in leadership and known for his work on 360-degrees-feedback. His singular ability to get results for top leaders has drawn over 150 CEOs and their management teams to address change in the workplace.*

Third: Dreams, and

Fourth: to give something of value to the society and to have a life mission.

For me it is clear that we do not have to wait for the end of our lives to have this realisation. We can start now, yesterday, the day before yesterday, last week, a decade ago or preferably when we are born.

Controlling your needs

You probably know Maslow's hierarchy of needs[14]. This hierarchy is often portrayed in the shape of a pyramid with the largest and the most fundamental needs at the bottom whereas the need for self-actualization and self-transcendence at the top.

The most fundamental and basic four layers of the pyramid contain what Maslow called "deficiency needs" or "d-needs": esteem, friendship and love, security, and physical needs. If these "deficiency needs" are not met – except for the most fundamental (physiological) need 'LOVE' – there may not be a physical indication, but the individual will feel anxious and tense.

Maslow's theory suggests that the most basic level of needs must be met before the individual will strongly desire - or focus motivation upon - the secondary or higher-level needs. Maslow also coined the term "meta-motivation" to describe the motivation of people who go beyond the scope of the basic needs and strive for constant betterment.

So how would you answer the question of regret?

Do you have any regrets so far?

I invite you to decide now what you will do to avoid regrets in the future.

You still have time - I am probably at the midday of my life, as I

---

14. *Maslow's hierarchy of needs is a theory in psychology proposed by Abraham Maslow in his 1943 paper "A Theory of Human Motivation" in Psychological Review.*

like to call it, but I was able to make changes.

Did you get around to do everything you wanted to do or are you still desperately seeking something? Do you have a sense of missing out on all kinds of experiences you ought to cherish? If this is you, keep reading and you might find something that you have been looking for, for a long time.

You do not have control over your last day on earth, but you do have control over the days leading up to that last one. At the end of this chapter, you will have learnt how to get to the end of your life feeling completely at peace because you lived 100% happy.

When I was hurt again and again I experienced something inside of me, a deep insight or a deep calling. This was the moment my transformation started.

My wakeup call was after I got laid off. Now I consider it to be the best thing that has happened to me. The universe had been sending me signals but I did not listen until I was laid off again. The desire was very small in the beginning as I mentioned in Chapter One in regards to The Law of Seeds.

The desire grew stronger and stronger. I wanted to change the way I would spend the rest of my life and this desire became stronger when my mother died. The death of my mother made me decide to write this book. The decision was made in an instant.

How to deal with the loss of someone you loved

You can consider life to be a rollercoaster and 2017 was quite a rollercoaster for me. My mother passed away in June. I know that for a lot of you and especially when you reach the age of fifty and older, parents become vulnerable as they reach the end of their lives. Grief makes a deep impact on us. Sometimes it can even overwhelm us or dominate our mood for years to come. It can teach us something or make us aware of something major. Looking within me I realised that my mother gave me a message to spread my wings and fly and to share the message; the message of our family, our tragedy, our love for each other. But also fear, the fear of not being ourselves and not always speaking our truth.

My grandmother passed away in 1978 when I was thirteen years old because of an immediate heart attack. She suffered through much grief after the death of my grandfather that she died within a week after his death. The grief was just too much for her to cope with. She could not or did not realise that his death was not only a big loss but could also have been a message or a situation to get out of. Maybe he wanted her to live on and cherish the memories she had of him and celebrate life much like he did. The grief overtook her. The message seemingly was not there for her, unfortunately.

Consider when you last were faced with the loss of a loved one. Or if you haven't experienced the trauma; think back on a major heart break, disappointment or misfortune you encountered in your past. How did it feel? How did you cope with it at that very moment? What kind of feelings did you have? Were you pushing your feelings away Were you in denial or did you express them in any way?

You know that expressing and depressing are very close to one another. Expressing your feelings is healthy. Not expressing your feelings might lead to depression. Be sure to express your emotions and not as a victim in any manner, but just by talking about how you feel. Expressing and depressing is like love and fear that are also closely connected. If you do not express your emotions or you push them as back you will never heal from your grief. When you want to cry, cry! When you want to smile, smile!

In some cultures, the death of a loved one is considered to be a celebration and people are dressed in white instead of black. They are smiling and celebrating. They celebrate the marvellous life of the deceased. Imagine that your loved one is looking over your shoulder now and he or she is only seeing your grief, your sadness, your negative emotions. Is that the response you really want to give? I don´t think so. So, embrace the death of your loved one and be free of the grief of this tragedy. If you focus on this tragedy sitting at home, thinking and overthinking why it all happened, it will only get worse. This also counts for a big disappointment or misfortune. It is the same mechanism.

The Law of Attraction says your thoughts will be your reality. When you go out and look at the signs in nature it will be the best way to start to heal. When my mother passed away there were several steps of healing. After the death of somebody you love, you first must accept that you are in grief and feel bad. Take your time and after a while go out into nature and look at the signs of nature.

Sounds weird?

I will give you an example from my own experience. First, I was very pleased that I made a beautiful speech at my mother's funeral. Because of my deep grief I realised that it was almost impossible for me to write something and present it too, but I did. It showed how resilient I could be. A couple of days after the funeral I thought the world entire had stopped. Everything had stopped! When I returned to the Netherlands my grief was so strong that everything became silent and

---

15. *Simply put, the Law of Attraction is the ability to attract into our lives whatever we are focusing on. It is believed that regardless of age, nationality or religious belief, we are all susceptible to the laws which govern the Universe, including the Law of Attraction - source: http://www.thelawofattraction.com/what-is-the-law-of-attraction/*

intense feelings of sadness overwhelmed me. It was like I disappeared in some thick mist; being numbed, disoriented and depressed.

I then started to look at the signs of nature. Well, it was not something I was conscious of. It just happened. Nature presents itself, just like that. When I came back from Brno, The Czech republic instead to the Netherlands, I saw butterflies everywhere. I never noticed butterflies in that way. Now suddenly they were there, lots of them, day in and day out.

It all looked like new life coming from everywhere, it was beautiful and breath taking. It was magical. I also saw the image of my mother over and over again. Curiously enough I saw feathers everywhere. I saw feathers on my doorstep, in the garden, on the beach, when I walked in the countryside, in the forest. I saw feathers all over the place. To me the butterflies and feathers were signs from my mother telling me to continue the work she had not finished in her life. It was an invitation to speak up and to pass on her message.

You really ought to express your emotions because it is important for your healing. Healing will make sure that you start living again with a big smile on your face. It is very important to go out and realise that you only have one life in this physical world. The universe is eternal and death is only a transition. Once you die you leave your body, but the soul and energy last.

I believe I have a very old soul because I was born in Egypt. I truly believe that there is something like an old soul within me. So, when you know that death is only a transition and you know that your energy is your own expression of your true self, take your time and express it. Death is only a transition from the human body to the infinite soul. Embracing who and what you are, is the most important chapter in your life. Your loved one who has passed away want to see you smile and go out; go into nature, learn from nature, learn how to be free of your negative thoughts, learn from animals and continue to live.

As I pointed out, I saw butterflies everywhere and I also saw them at my mother's home the very same day after she died. For me these are the symbols of my mother. Like ladybirds are symbols of my father. When my second daughter was born I saw lady birds around her bed, in her room. It was exactly a year after my father's passing. Isn't that beautiful? Isn't it wonderful that you know that your loved one is still with you? Don't see it as a tragedy; see it as a transition from the bodily life to the infinite being. The soul is still there. Remember the journey is the destination. Go ahead with your journey, embrace your life and be happy with what you have and who and what you are – your precious self, finding your own purpose in life.

Transformation. Turning into a butterfly

Going through my transformation was very difficult because change has never been easy. I started to explore the connections and relationships I had. I discovered that some of them did not serve me at all – I had to terminate those relationships. They sucked the energy right out of me.

It got rid of the habit of waking up at night filled with anxiety at the thought of growing old without a soulful connection. Living as a desperate woman after fifty.

I took a close look at my life when I turned fifty and realised I did not want to go the same way following that same familiar path over and over again. This was all consuming and destroying my dreams and my life. I did not want to die with a foggy mind that never allowed me to explore all the things I always wanted to do.

As I became conscious of what I was doing and I changed the negative pattern, my mind-set took to changing and this happened during my Quantum Success study in the United States. The discovery of the power of affirmations contributed greatly to my transformation. I read affirmations day after day after day. Slowly I started to notice changes. My energy was growing. I started to perceive the world in a totally unique way. Gratitude became my travelling companion. It was like it had always been there and I just missed it. I knew it would never leave me again.

Every day I started with new habits. These new habits were sometimes quite difficult. Scientific neurological research[16] shows that you need to be committed to applying these new habits for forty days in a row. Only then you will be able to integrate them in your daily lifestyle forever.

It is so challenging especially considering that our brain rejects any shift in pattern. But this shift with affirmations and gratitude sweetens your life. It's worth it!

---

16. *Psycho-Cybernetics, A New Way to Get More Living Out of Life, by Maxwell Maltz. Although a plastic surgeon he was one of the first to notice that people require a minimum of 21 days to form a new habit. Further studies by many others have shown that based on the type of habit, people require 21-40 days or sometimes up to a year to fully embrace a new habit.*

The Law of Gratitude

'Walk as if you are kissing the Earth with your feet.'

- Thích Nhat Hanh

Gratitude leads to greatness. It can literally turn what you have into more than enough. It turns jobs to joy, chaos into order, uncertainty unto clarity and peace to an otherwise chaotic day. Need I say more?

The Law of Gratitude[17] consists of four rules;

1. The more you are in a state of gratitude the more you will attract things to be grateful for.

    Be grateful for what you have and you will end up having more.

    Focus on what you do not have and you will never have enough.

2. Being happy won't always make you grateful but being grateful will always make you happy.

    It's nearly impossible to sincerely appreciate a moment and frown about it at the same time.

    To be happy right now does not mean you do not desire more, it means you're grateful for what you have and patient for what is yet to come.

3. Gratitude fosters true forgiveness which is when you can sincerely say, "Thank you for the experience."

    It makes no sense to condemn or regret an important life lesson.

    Gratitude makes sense of yesterday, brings peace to the present, and creates a positive vision for tomorrow.

17. *The Hidden Power of Universal Laws - PsiTek*

4. You never need for more than you have at any given moment.

It has been said that the highest form of prayer is giving thanks. Instead of praying 'for' things, give thanks for what you already have. Are you breathing or not? If your answer is yes and I am sure you do, you should be grateful for that.

When life gives you every reason to be negative, think of one good reason to be positive. There's always something to be grateful for.

To integrate this law into your daily life I highly recommend keeping a journal.

Write down at least three things you're grateful for.

Each day at dawn.

Be Grateful

What are you grateful for?

As said, every morning when I wake up I write down what I am grateful for and why.

I invite you to write down at least 3 things every morning you are grateful for.

To give you some examples;

- I'm grateful for my health – I nearly died, actually several times in my life. The first time was in Egypt when I was two years old and laid haplessly for two weeks with a terrible fever as hot as forty-one degrees. My father told me when I was a bit older that I was believed to be dead, but that it was a miracle that after two weeks of high fever I recovered from what was thought to be dengue fever.

- The second near-death experience was when I was almost raped at the age of twelve. Yes, I am grateful I am alive and healthy. I am also grateful for the wisdom of both of my parents and for the journeys across the world that changed my life several times.

- I almost died emotionally when I got divorced and I had to fight as a working mother in a management position abroad far from my beautiful country, far away from my old friends, far away from my parents to support me. Taking care of my two daughters all by myself. Especially when I got fired or when the company I worked for closed.

I sent hundreds of application letters to get a position on the same level as in Czechoslovakia. It was not easy. Once, when I came through three interviews within one company they made me wait for three weeks to decide whether I was hired or not. After three weeks I was told another candidate had been selected. They told me I had not been able to show them who I truly was. I was so different. I did not fit. I did not understand this at that time, but now I do. Back then I could not sympathise in any way with that kind of culture and the kind of society full of hidden truths and acting masks. Now I can be grateful for this experience. It contributed to my liberation.

Chapter V

Abundance, self-image and self-love

As I began to love myself
I freed myself of anything
that is no good for my health
- food, people, things, situations,
and everything that drew me down
and away from myself.
At first, I called this attitude
a healthy egoism.
Today I know it is "LOVE OF ONESELF"

-Charlie Chaplin, April 16th, 1959 on his 70th Birthday

The Law of Abundance

How do we know that we experience abundance?

Let me explain what abundance means by using an instance from my own experience. Considering my training and history as a procurement manager, if I should have had a clear vision of who I wanted to be and what I truly wanted in life and my career; I immediately would have taken action in what I can only describe as a 'flow'. An inspired tide of consistency between my vision and my reality. I would find immense success and experience abundance because of this very 'flow'.

Imagine another person with the same background and training but not having a clear 'why', a clear vision about the future of what she or he truly desires to accomplish. You would immediately notice this person to be leading an uninspired life. Living without 'flow' or lasting energy. Such a person would totally depend on direct instructions from others without having any conviction in his or her role. Take away the instructions from the manager and he or she would not be able to do anything. This way the person would not experience success nor abundance.

Most people act as such in our society. Especially when you observe people operating in business. People who start in existing businesses offer products and services that are not unique. Competitors are copied, or they try to come up with some new offer that seems different but is still the very same. This goes on and on.

Abundance has nothing to do with your background or training, rather it has everything to do with being who you envision yourself to be. While doing so never emulate or copy someone else. Do not try to keep up appearances trying to look good or avoid looking bad. Avoiding these traps will get you into the infinite possibilities and opportunities that simmer deep inside you.

Critically examine yourself in your workplace. Some questions to help you with that are:

Are you doing what will take you to the place where you envision yourself in the future?

Will it make you successful?

And what is the definition of success for you?

Is it consistent with your true self?

Your biggest success in life is being and feeling happy and especially, happiness that comes from being your true self. Many have told me that when they wanted to be themselves, they would get into problems at their workplace. That means they are not in the right workplace. Sadly enough, we can play the role of marionettes and puppets our whole lives without knowing how great life could have been. When people find themselves doing what they really do not want to do, they start pretending they have no other option. Through this pretence they drift away from their true selves.

I hear this often when I talk to my friends, clients or others about their choices. Many maintain they have no choice or control over their own circumstances. That is only because they are not connected with their true selves and they really do not know anything about the law of abundance. If you say, 'I have no choice', it is at first only your thought and nothing more. However, holding on to that thought makes it your destination. I know that everybody deserves love and more so as to be who he or she truly is.

You are unique and just like we are different as human beings so are our challenges. Sometimes you may think your journey in life is filled with many more struggles and challenges than others. But how we choose to deal with our challenges is what makes our story extraordinary or unique; the more challenges we overcome the greater our story. This book is about how you can overcome your extraordinary struggles.

You are making choices all the time and the outcome of these choices is your present reality. So, whether it is the decisions you overthink or the decision you make in 17 seconds (these 17 seconds are based on an exercise from the book 'Ask and its given'[18]). Your thoughts determine who you are and is known to be one of the universal laws. To support this, I would like to mention the words of a great teacher:

"In the absence of That Which You Are Not, That Which You ARE...Is NOT." – Neale Donald Walsch[19]

---

18 *Ask and It Is Given is the bestselling book by Esther and Jerry Hicks on the teachings of Abraham. It gives us 22 different powerful processes to achieve our goals. No matter where we are, there's a process that can make our lives better. Although the Law of Attraction became popular through the film "The Secret", Ester and Jerry hicks have been working on the theory for almost 20 years prior.*
19 *Taken from "Parable of The Little Soul" by Neale Donald Walsch*

Take a moment to understand what he is saying. It took me a while but then it hit me like a lightning bolt.

Exercise abundance

This is a visualisation exercise.

When I start to visualise, especially visualizing something that is beautiful or something I desire it delights me, inspires me, fills me with joy and gives me hope. This is what abundance feels like to me.

Can I invite you to experience the same?

Put yourself in a comfortable position and think of something beautiful or something meaningful to you – a flower, the sun, a hug, a child playing, your loved one or whatever makes you feel happy or joyful. Think about it for at least 17 seconds. Prolong to 68 seconds. As stated you need this much time to make a permanent imprint in your subconsciousness mind. Measure the time. You can repeat this exercise whenever you want. I'm sure you will want to repeat it once you experience the effect the first time.

This exercise is very powerful to shift your energy into abundance and your state of being to your desired direction.

I decided a couple of years ago, that I wanted to create a powerful new and abundant self-image.

When I started my transformation, the first lesson I learnt was that instead of doing, we have to BE.

What you give is what you get!

People do not realise that "Being" is the basic criterion for your abundant self-image. So how do you see yourself most of the time? Do you see yourself as a person who forever struggles and never succeeds? Or as a person who is unloved? This self-image that is based on limitation and fear will eventually become your reality. You then do not even need to experience these circumstances first hand for them to become your reality. By thinking in the manner you do is how you will perceive the world which will directly reflect in your mood and behaviour.

However, let me ask you the opposite. How do you see yourself in the mirror of self-love? Your self-image will attract an equivalent response from the universe. So, if you see yourself as a person struggling all the time, the universe will respond by making opportunities scarce and you will find yourself stuck in perpetual struggle. If you see yourself as someone blessed with options and divine choices in your life, the universe will present you a lot of opportunities and you will feel blessed and abundant in that reality.

I often reply to people who tell me that they have no time or control over their choices in life and that they are actually very simply giving instructions to the universe. Instructions transmitted through their thoughts to take away their control over time and their choices in life. They are in fact saying to themselves 'I have no time for you because I have got so many things to do.' I wonder what are these 'many things'? Mostly, they are things we strive for to do instead of striving to "BE" and enjoy an abundant life with healthy relationships with ourselves and others.

Remember: whatever you constantly broadcast through your thoughts, beliefs and feelings is what will manifest in your life. This will mould your self-image.

Sometimes people recognize the need to change but then they think it is the responsibility of someone else to change them. Or they want to change and become like someone else, copy some role model. This is however a misconception. You are the only one who has the power to change yourself on your own terms to become that unique version of you. Unlike no one else.

Let me demonstrate this by using an exercise. The exercise can help you change your self-image. By changing what you think about yourself, you can instantly change who you are because who you are is a combination of your thoughts and your beliefs and your habits. These three factors combined create the person you are. Not only because they are closely connected with each other but more importantly because they feed your behaviour. The person you are about to become, caused by these three factors is a process that already started when you were about six years old.

As I mentioned previously, your self-image becomes your reality and what you think about most of the time and believe about yourself forms your self-image. For example, you will find yourself always short of money, because money is an energy which is attracted to or repelled by the thoughts that you have about yourself. If you want your financial circumstances to change, begin with changing the thoughts.

Now before you go further (I promised you an exercise), I want to emphasise that you do not need to change any aspect of your life that you are happy with. So if you are happy just having ten euros in your pocket, that is fine. Everybody feels abundance in a different way. And even if you want more money but do not feel the energy, that power within yourself or you do not feel an emotional connection in your solar plexus (the place right under your chest where most nerve fibres radiate in your body); you won't get any corresponding result. The results you get are signals you transmit through your feelings to the universe and the universe will give an exact response to these feelings.

It is therefore crucial to be aware of what your self-image is.

Are you constantly heeding to someone else's opinion of you? Asking yourself whether you're good enough? Wondering if you will ever become as good as others are? I did the same in the past, comparing myself with others, trying to keep up appearances or live up to the expectations others had of me. It does not matter how old you are, you can change and improve any aspect of your self-image. Anybody can!

How do you create a new abundant self-image? First of all, you need to understand your wrong beliefs. Are the beliefs you have about yourself true? Remember, all your fears and habits contribute to your current self-image.

It is time to decide to change your beliefs. Of course, you are the only one who can make this decision for and about yourself.

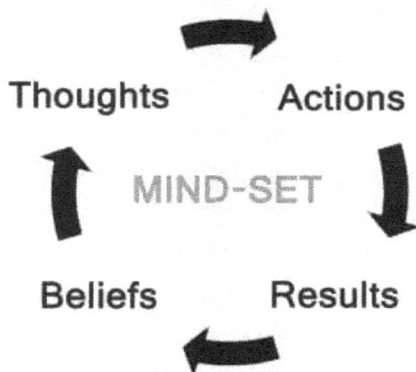

Thoughts → **Actions**

↑ MIND-SET ↓

Beliefs ← **Results**

As the model shows, each thought is fed by a belief. Thoughts turn into actions, actions into results and results into beliefs. Whether something worked for you or not, doesn't really matter. This model is the bases of the behaviour of every human on this planet.

If things go wrong you create a limiting belief. If things go well you create an empowering belief. This goes on and on in a cycle. Nothing you can do about, can you?

Well of course you can! If you can change your mind-set into a positive, self-loving and abundant mind set your thoughts will immediately be transformed accordingly. And so, the model does its work; only now in a positive, reinforcing way. Nice isn't it? It was an amazing experience when I first discovered this.

Practical example; if you do not want to BE that person who has to be careful about every euro that is spent (an example about money is of course the easiest way to demonstrate how this works), you need to start to become a person (mind-set) who can confidently spend money without guilt.

This could apply to those divorced considering I experienced this myself as have many others. Of course, it is obvious! When people divorce they understandably tend to focus on being able to keep fulfilling their own basic needs. Moreover, in marriage two people are responsible for keeping the finances solid. After a divorce, all of a sudden each individual becomes an independent entity and it includes being financial responsible as well.

After my divorce, although I was always financially independent, I felt guilty spending money because my behaviour was fed by an old limiting belief. A belief I inherited from my mother. She talked a lot about the scarcity of money and that you had to be careful about spending. Therefore, I would always ask myself if I really needed that certain item or product I was about to buy or if it was just my ego that wanted it. I was confused. Not my true self. Not able to use my common sense. Not being able to see things clearly for what they were.

Would you like to attract more money? Would you like to feel comfortable when spending it? Do you believe in the effortless and the infinite abundance of the universe? Do you believe in your own strong self-image? Those two beliefs are the keys.

I promised you an exercise. So, finally, here it is.

Exercise self-image

How would you describe a person living in the realm of infinite abundance?

Challenging question?

No sweat.

The answer(s) will come.

1. Close your eyes for at least 17 seconds and prolong it to 68 seconds (yes, again). Visualise an abundant self-image; how would you describe this self-image? Do not overcomplicate it. Just see yourself standing somewhere in a certain way.

2. Begin to affirm with words (say out loud while keeping your eyes shut) all the wonderful things you would love to have (material and immaterial). Keep your self-image in your mind.

3. To make your self-image more powerful, use self-affirmations, begin each sentence with 'I am'. We now concentrate on being that self-image.

I am ....
(insert a word or phrase to describe the image you want to adopt)

Some examples are:

I am beautiful, I am wealthy, I am healthy, I am abundant, I am special, I am extraordinary, I am great, I am fabulous, I am successful, I am very talented, I am a very good speaker and so on and forth.

Audrey Hepburn (a famous actress from the old days) once said "Nothing's impossible". The word impossible itself says 'I'm possible!'. In the same way, nobody is imperfect. The word says, 'I'm perfect!' Funny and remarkable isn't it?

Imperfection means that you are perfect to the degree
you see yourself as perfect.
Give yourself some time to let this sentence sink in.

When you say the words 'I am' and you affix the proper noun to the phrase, you are forming a new self-image. Neurologically speaking you are training your brain. You are telling your brain directly to make new lasting connections. Connections that will direct new choices and new behaviour. Magical isn't it? It's the magic of using your self-consciousness.

A force which develops itself at an early age. At the age of two to three. That self-consciousness makes you aware that you are a someone with a body and certain traits. You recognise yourself in the mirror for the first time. You recognise there are others. You recognise there are objects. You start to develop language to identify the things around you. It makes you aware of yourself and others. That same power can be used to train your brain to be aware of what you are doing. It is like a magical force you can switch on and off.

You have to repeat the 'I am' - statements to yourself and write them down because these statements are crucial for your self-image. When you say these words frequently they become your own truth. Say them at least the first forty days. As mentioned, this is the period it takes for you and your brain to adopt your new habits.

Don't worry about noticing any changes – all you need to make yourself accountable for is repeating these words every day. Simple and easily done. No effort required. They could be the first words you repeat to yourself when you wake up in the morning.

Remember to write them down. Words gain more power when you stand up and affirm 'I am abundant'. You may feel funny at first (that's alright of course). Invest true feeling into the words; stand on your feet and repeat the words loudly. First in front of a mirror and later to an audience if you like. When you start to feel an inner shift, this habit will become yours and a mental and emotional shift will truly begin to occur from within.

Recap

Complete the following sentences (make as many sentences as you like):

I am ....

I am ....

I am ....

I am ....

I am ....

Take a few minutes for each sentence. You can use one word or a phrase. Some more examples include: I am trusting, I am deserving, I am respected, I am beautiful, I am attractive, I am fabulous, I am wealthy, I am healthy, I am grateful, I am clever and talented; I am confident and funny; I am open-minded, I am brilliant, I am loving, I am expanding, I am wise, generous, and relaxed. I am optimistic, I am helpful, I am ready, I am effective, I am powerful, I am strong and balanced; I'm extraordinary, I'm capable, I'm focused.

How can you love yourself 100%?

What does self-love even mean?

A lot of us have low self-esteem because we are comparing ourselves to others. We do so constantly and consistently. Our education and upbringing are mainly focussed on becoming a better version of ourselves when in fact we are already the greatest version of ourselves. Let me ask you a question to illustrate this. Did you ever attend an exam which was assessed focusing on the correct answers?

No, it never happened. Did it? The things you would notice were the red underlined pieces of text that were wrong or you would notice the marked errors. You are trained to never ever be good enough.

Comparing ourselves to others leads to never being good enough. You can never be as good as another person. It's simply a different individual and therefore, simply not possible to be like him or her. If you still try and emulate them, the results would only upset you further.

For instance, you can easily become upset about nothing at all. It is caused by some internal contraction or unfulfilled desire to never be able to live up to the image of another. This energy leads to, for instance, impulsively buying a new pair of shoes (or a lot more than that) or eating lots of chocolate. After that, guilt or shame is what's left. Guilty for spending all that money on yourself or feeling ashamed about over treating yourself with something delightful.

I used to listen to the opinions of others. Repeatedly comparing and listening to someone else's opinion is a sign we do not love ourselves. We conform to society's expectations of us. In that way, we are controlled by those expectations that are not ours.

We already have a lot of troubles to live up to our own expectations.
So why should we add the expectations others have of us?
That doesn't make sense. Or does it?

We have our own self-expectations, but the case is that we are often influenced by the expectations of others and as a result, live someone else's life and not our own.

Let me illustrate. At work, your boss asks you to do something that you do not like, or you disagree with (because your values and talents are out of line with that), but you do it anyway because you are afraid to be fired. With kids at home and a mortgage to pay, I had to do all that was possible to survive – even if it meant doing things I did not like or disagreed with. Under such circumstances, do you think that it is possible to love yourself 100%?

You are modelling yourself into what is expected of you. Even if it does not suit your inner being, does not suit your talents or does not suit your values. If you find yourself constantly unhappy about your workplace, it simply means you are not doing what you love. If you are doing what you love, it won't ever feel like work.

The next lesson is one that I learned from several great teachers such as Louise Hay[20], Robert Holden[21] and Wayne Dyer[22].

It's easy to say you love yourself when you wake up in the morning. But when you look in the mirror as you brush your teeth, what do you see when you look into your own eyes? Do you see someone doing the things that bring self-fulfilment and happiness? Are you in love with your imperfections – your big nose or ears, hairy legs, freckles and spots, everything about you? Or is there some nagging dissatisfaction about how you look? Oh, and of course it is healthy to laugh about yourself every now and then. Self-mockery is a good thing.

You need to get to the point where you embrace your imperfections. Nobody is perfect - neither me, nor you or anybody else. This also applies to the fashion models you see in magazines or on the catwalk. You would think they love themselves 100%, but then you hear a tragic case of suicide or anorexia or bulimia. A result of being driven by someone else's expectations about them. What's beauty worth if you do not know what true beauty is? And can it be neutral or is it objective or subjective?

---

20. *Louise Hay was a speaker, healer, artist and author of the book "You can heal your life"*
21. *Robert Holden (born 1965) is a British psychologist, author, and broadcaster who works in the field of positive psychology and well-being and is considered "Britain's foremost expert on happiness".*
22. *Wayne Walter Dyer (1940 – 2015) was an American philosopher, self-help author, and a motivational speaker. His first book, Your Erroneous Zones (1976), is one of the best-selling books of all time with an estimated 35 million copies sold to date.*

Do you often go for a walk to savour nature? Do you exercise to nourish your mind and body? Do you listen to your favourite music or do you often sit in front of a television that feeds you lies about your self-image? The word 'television' contains the word 'vision'; your true vision can be muddled by television. Turn off the television and go out to explore nature - watch animals, and as you do so, explore the feelings deep in your heart and solar plexus as you ask yourself: am I being who I love or am I doing what someone else loves? Am I fulfilling my own vision or that of others?

I used to be a victim of trying to please everybody because I felt like an outsider. I had to get everyone to like me by pleasing all of them. I was trying to bridge a huge infinite gap.

To love yourself doesn't mean you are a narcissist. It's okay if your friends think differently when you decide that the best option for you is to stay indoors and not attend a party. It's also okay to come up with great ideas to change your career that everyone else considers to be unreal. Don't worry about it, because their reaction to your 'self-love' may be based on their own flawed self-image or fear. They are only jealous.

In respect to self-love, I stopped being competitive and watched as things started to happen for me – good things came my way just the way I dreamt. In the past I was very competitive; in our society lots of contract opportunities and processes are based on one's skills, so we fight and compete eternally to improve our skills and outpace one another. We compete to stand out in the market place offering only a better version of the same or a better sameness. Through this we will never know peace.

When you stop being competitive and start becoming who you really want to be, you will experience happiness. All of us in our darkest moments are looking for light and for the truth. But quite often we pursue our light through drugs, or by overeating or by spending time in the wrong companionship. Because of this we feed emptiness and dissatisfaction even more as these things won't satisfy us anymore.

If we see how these mechanisms work, we stop abusing ourselves. Destruction will cease immediately.

Self-love affirmation/meditation

This meditation will help you to get rid of feelings of unworthiness and replace them with a powerful sense of self-love. If you say the affirmations with strong and positive emotions while directing feelings of love and kindness towards yourself, there will be a change in your perspective and your self-image.

Shall we begin?

You can do this in front of a mirror or if that is not possible you can simply say it out loud. I will give you a wide range of affirmations.:

I love myself. I really love myself.

I am a great person just the way I am.

I am already in love with myself.

I am happy, I am proud and beautiful.

I am proud to live a life in abundance.

I deserve to be happy.

I truly love myself, I am glad to be me.

I am glad I am alive, I am proud of my beauty.

I deserve to live in abundance.

I deserve to be happy, healthy, and successful.

I am successful.

I give myself permission to be happy, healthy and wealthy.

I give myself permission to have the things I want.

I give myself permission to be treated well.

I give myself permission to feel good.

I am good enough already.

I am great, and my greatness doesn't depend on what anybody says.

How I look like and what I do is good enough.

I have already accomplished enough because I am enough.

I am worthy because I exist, because I breathe.

I know my own value and my own boundaries.

I celebrate who I am because I truly love myself.

When I look deep in to my eyes, I can say I truly love myself.

I believe in myself because this is my own truth and existence in the present moment.

After these affirmations you can take a deep breath. Breathe in and out and if you can repeat the exercise at least for a couple of minutes each day you will find yourself in a wonderful feeling of love.

As Esther Hicks[23], states in her book about the law of attraction ("Ask and it is given"):

"When we appreciate ourselves, we empower ourselves with energy. The highest level of appreciation is self-appreciation, and this will guarantee love and happiness."

---

23. *Esther Hicks is an American inspirational speaker and author. She has co-written nine books with her husband Jerry Hicks, presented numerous workshops on the law of attraction and appeared in the original version of the 2006 film The Secret.*

Why self-love is so important

Let's further explore the idea of self-love and how beneficial self-love is.

Until now, we've explored how you can love yourself for 100%. Now, I will explain why self-love is so important.

When I went to London, I bought a perfume at the airport and I found the inspiration for this topic in that experience. The name of the perfume was "It's good to be bad". Don't get me wrong, I do not mean we have to be bad to be good (well, we can be naughty every now and then), but it is sometimes good to put yourself first and be honest about it.

Most of us grew up in environments where if we wanted something beautiful like a nice pair of shoes, we were told we had to be nice and well behaved. I grew up with the idea fully engrained in me, a belief worsened by growing up in a communist society. Sit in the corner, shut up and behave – and appreciate what's coming to you. That is what the communist society valued and rewarded – docile sheep that hunkered in a corner and accepted whatever was tossed at them.

This kind of threatening conditioning (if-you-do-this-you-will-get-that) bred destructive thoughts in countless people, especially women who were taught that they could not put themselves in the first place in any way. I am not claiming that society is entirely responsible for creating that distorted self-image, but society does play an important part in how a child's self-image develops and evolves.

During the communist era, the mental conditioning was such that you were only worth something if you got good grades at school and studied at a university. Mostly amplified by parents who were disappointed by their own way of life. Luckily, I was able to attend university although and unfortunately, not in any Western country.

The requirement was getting good grades in school and learning to suppress my desires. There was low tolerance for individuality, mental advancement or spirituality or religion of any sort. You also had to be a member of a proactive communist party to be admitted to university.

I remember how a girl sitting next to me was punished. She was sent home because she wore a T-shirt with an American flag on it. I found this truly frustrating. When I was fifteen years old, I wasn't allowed to wear any make-up because everyone had to conform to a standard of behaviour. One girl in our class had to go to the bathroom to remove her make-up. I never forgot this experience.

The teacher was not aware she put her self-esteem and confidence at the lowest level. Nowadays, in the Western education system educators and education inspectors strive for mediocrity. Highly talented kids or kids with any special talent and passion are mostly out of place. Excellence or uniqueness is not an asset. It's another way to low self-esteem and confidence but it all comes down to the same thing.

I like the slogan: *"Good girls go to heaven, but bold girls will go everywhere"*[24].

When I first came to the Netherlands, I did not know anything about self-love right through the period I got married, gave birth to my kids and when I started my new career abroad. I wondered: why is it that some people can love themselves and others cannot? And why is it that we are not taught how to be self-loving, anyway?

I realise it all depends on the kind of childhood we experienced and what kind of beliefs our parents and educators passed on to us, imprinted into our subconscious mind. I remember the time when I was young. How happy I could be with just one tiny white daisy. I would pick a white daisy and start picking the petals of the flower while chanting repeatedly, 'he loves me, he loves me not' right until the last petal presented me with the answer. That answer meant so much to me.

---

24. *Taken from the 1993 song "Good girls go to heaven" by Meat Loaf.*

There are only two choices: to live in fear or to live in love. When you choose to live in fear, you won't be able to follow your dreams. You bury your dreams in a grave alongside your talents by doing so. When I was still a child, sitting in a meadow was all that I wanted to do surrounded by all these lovely daisies. I could do this 'he-loves-me-he-loves-me-not' for days. To me, it was like living in love.

Gradually, I stopped validating outside of me; instead, I started looking inside. I started to dive deeper within myself to find self-validation. This shift was not easy and it won't be easy for you, but I assure you it will be a magical shift.

You know that anything can happen because you have trust. You have the power within yourself. You trust yourself from the inside. It is much like self-love. It all begins with understanding and then loving yourself. In self-love you know that you can conquer anything and it doesn't matter if you are alone or with someone else. Because the more powerful you are, the stronger you are from within. You know that the world makes you more beautiful and you make the world more beautiful. And this is my mission - to inspire you with this book, to give you support and to make you understand that everything is possible – no matter what your age is.

"There are two basic motivating forces: fear and love. When we are afraid, we pull back from life. When we are in love, we open to all that life has to offer with passion, excitement, and acceptance. We need to learn to love ourselves first, in all our glory and our imperfections. If we cannot love ourselves, we cannot fully open to our potential to create. Evolution and all hopes for a better world rest in the fearlessness and open-hearted vision of people who embrace life"

– John Lennon[25]

25 *John Lennon (1940 – 1980) was an English singer, songwriter, and peace activist who co-founded the Beatles, the most commercially successful band in the history of popular music.*

Chapter VI

Finding purpose through finding yourself

"For the past 33 years, I have looked in the mirror every morning and asked myself: "If today was the last day of my life, would I want to do what I am about to do today?" And whenever the answer has been "No" for too many days in a row, I knew I needed to change something. Almost everything – all external expectations, all pride, all fear of embarrassment or failure – these things just fall away in the face of death leaving only what is truly important. Remembering that you are going to die is the best way I know to avoid the trap of thinking you have something to lose."

- Steve Jobs [26]

The queue, Czechoslovakia 1982

It is a cold, miserable grey day. It's raining and snowing at the same time. Brno is colourless. People pass each other without any sense of direction and without any expression on their face. Humanity and 'joie de vivre' are gone. It's almost Christmas. Time to go to town, vessels with carp have delivered their precious cargo. Carp is the Czech

26 *Steven Jobs was an American entrepreneur, business magnate, inventor and industrial designer. He was the chairman, chief executive officer (CEO), and a co-founder of Apple Inc.*

fish for Christmas, a tradition which is curiously enough retrieved from the Jews.

I am with Jana, my "big" sister, to go to town together. Not to buy carp, the day before Christmas is still early enough to buy carp. Fresh carp it must be at Christmas for us. We Czechs eat the whole fish, you know. My father makes soup from the head and the rest is baked and eaten. The scales are removed. It is customary for Czechs to put a scale in their wallet for luck. But for now, my sister and I are focused on getting oranges. Yes, oranges!

We walk through the city with a glimmer of hope that something special is being sold somewhere. We're lucky. There is a long queue in front of a store in which they sell a small range of fruit and vegetables. All these people who are lined up are certainly not there getting the regular stuff from that store. Something special is on sale today.

We both try hard to see what's being sold. But we can't figure it out from a distance. We decide to join the queue. Behind us other people queue up. They ask us what's being sold. We do not know, nor do the people in front of us. I choose to leave the queue, asking Jana to keep my spot, and to try to get more in front of the row to finally know what's being sold. To my surprise I find out they sell oranges and bananas. Extraordinary for us, for sure. And it is exactly what we went out for.

There is nothing else being sold other than the two choices at hand. But we are used to that. At least they sell something that is not a regular product for the store. We can get green or brown bananas. The oranges are dry, hmmm; but hey, take it or leave it. And who cares?! We stay in the cold. I shiver and I'm afraid to get sick again. We stay because we want that fruit so desperately.

Standing in a row is hardly pleasant at all. People do not talk, hold their position and wait for their turn. We look around and see glimpses of satisfied people with a big smile on their faces going home with a full bag of fruit. Being lucky enough to be able to give their children something healthy to eat that evening. We may soon be just as lucky.

To eat something different than the coconuts which for some reason were always available in the vegetable store. Probably they were part of some trade agreement with a developing country.

My toes are freezing slowly until I can't feel them anymore. I wonder whether they already turned blue. My sister makes strange comments about the long queue. She's clearly annoyed and that is an understatement. She's pissed off! Of course, showing this so loudly is not a wise thing to do especially in those days of oppression. Fortunately, the row in front of us is becomes shorter and shorter. I now get a view of the crates and boxes. Someone yells out that you no longer need to queue up because the merchandise is almost sold out. Nobody is listening and people are still queing up. They simply take the chance.

Somebody in front of us orders a kilogram of bananas. That isn't a social thing to do considering there isn't enough for everyone. There are now only two in front of us. We are getting close. Closer and closer. The delicacies however are gone. Sold out. The bananas and oranges are gone. Nothing is left. We stare at the empty boxes in disbelief. I am deeply disappointed, sad and angry. My sister even more so. We walk home with frozen feet, frustrated and outraged. At the same time, we face yet another day a 'dinner' of bread and sardines.

Life rules

This world and its inhabitants will change. These change processes are now in full swing. We are now all tested and trained from the start of the new Mayan calendar. The Mayan calendar points to the year 2012 in which a major shift in consciousness started to arise. Like a rebirth and transformation of our planet, to be able to enter a new age full of new challenges we have to master (challenges such as globalisation, climate issues, artificial intelligence, privacy issue and so on). Don't feel burdened by new possibilities which will present themselves. This is a century loping process.

There are no certainties or guarantees in this life, so do not expect them. Expect no bananas or oranges if there's a chance they will be sold out. What is possible is to set priorities again, choose wisely and be aware that there will be more multiple choices in your life which you can decide to follow or not. Life is an adventure, a journey through time. There is no end, simply a beginning.

Everything is moving and changing all the time. Therefore, move along in every day, week, month, year and follow your inner compass. See it like this: you live on a boat on the river that floats in clear running water from the fixed point of today to an unknown destination.

Live every chapter of your life to the fullest, insert a new energy flow in your life by making choices with head and heart together.

What will be your next chapter in life? You create your own destination. You reach your goal by learning to dare to embrace the unknown, live at the border of your possibilities and not at the outer borders of your insecurities. Be active, not passive and have an end in mind without holding on to it too tight (as Stephen Covey[27] said: *'Begin with the end in mind'*), focus on your goal but try to achieve it by taking small steps at a time. Be flexible and trust the ocean to be the captain of your own boat. Go with the flow and let the waves take you to your desired destination.

The most important aspect of your life is your soul. Your age doesn't matter. You can heal if you want. Then you can heal your frustration from pain and from the trauma of the past and present. Yes, even from your untrue thoughts about menopause or peno-pause. Be good to yourself.

When you are getting older you become a better student in living your life. You learn everyday so that you can give more love to others. You rewrite the story of yourself every day and gratefulness for so many lessons have now become your guide. The footprint you will leave behind will make an even deeper imprint. This is your heritage.

---

27 *Dr. Stephen R. Covey is the author of acclaimed books including the international best seller, The 7 Habits of Highly Effective People which has sold more than 25 million copies in 40 languages throughout the world.*

The Law of Life - life is an adventure

What's worth living for? Do you know? Perchance on New Year's Eve you are planning to go on a diet or you want to make a trip, or you want to start your own business. By the end of January, where are you then? What have you done to realise your intention?

During my transformation and my journey, I wrongfully thought my life's purpose was to stay in corporate business. Because of that I eventually got frustrated, sad and I lived in fear of a boss I really resented. It seems that is the way things work for most of us. You study, you find a job, you make a career, you buy a house, you get married, you have children and yet we do not have a clue about our life's purpose or our true desires.

I started to change and finally opened my eyes when I realised that the purpose of life and the purpose of living is joy, happiness and freedom. What changed me? When I started questioning myself and when I started reflecting on a lot of experiences and choices; I started to change. Many like me came home tired from work and turned on the television. They shut their own vision by watching television or by over consuming social media posts. It really shuts down your brain as well. And do not get me wrong. You do not have to turn off your television permanently but rather ask yourself every now and then, the three questions I give you at the end of this chapter.

What's happening in your life?

Do you like your job? How are your finances? How is your love life? How is your health? How long did the last relationship last? What was your childhood like?

You need to realise that these are important questions in life because these questions help you find your own journey – your very purpose. Most of our lives we think that life is difficult and filled with a lot of struggles. Of course, sometimes it is. But our mind-set can often create more complexities than there are. Then it becomes important, especially for women in their menopause is when life starts to be more and more challenging to truly get in control of life!

Your WHY

As stated, your age doesn't matter. More importantly, you need to ask yourself: what do I want? This is not referring to something like a new car or a house but a purpose in life, a destiny or a life's journey.

What's that thing? And WHY do you want it?

'Why' is the starting point of everything. It is your vision statement or mission in life. It fuels your daily actions. It gives you direction. It gives you something to hold on to. It is however also moving like you yourself are moving all the time. Your WHY will therefore move with you and within you. It is not some static motto or slogan. It keeps evolving like you evolve. Because of that, it is of great significance to fine-tune your WHY every now and then. You will discover that you will make slight changes rather than the big ones. Your WHY or mission at its core is already inside you your whole life. The core will remain the same.

It's crucial to recognise that finding your 'Why' becomes easier as soon as you forgive yourself and others, move away from old habits and integrate new habits in to your life.

Being approved or fulfilled?

Our lives are usually ordered by systems and are often a reaction to the circumstances in which we find ourselves: 'The boss likes me so I should be happy!' Psychologically speaking we seek for and live for the approval of others and what they think of us. We think that our key to happiness is how often the circumstances we find ourselves in are good to us.

So, think about why do you want, what you want. Is it because you can win the approval of others or is it because you can fulfil something truly important towards your destiny?

Embrace your 'why' as your truth and you will truly find happiness. We often need to ask ourselves why. Why do I want to have a happier relationship? Why do I want to have more money? Why do I want to be healthier? This is the key to a more successful life.

It's easy to blame our parents, our background, our past, our less privileged family or society for our pain and misery. However, this attitude must stop.

The first action is to write down what you want. Make sure you feel comfortable and at ease. Put on some of your favourite music, take a walk, meditate if you like, exercise even or do something that makes you feel wonderful. Your true feeling and thoughts will arise in that state.

Keep on writing, do not stop and keep coming back to your list. Add more to it and even more. Turn it into an extensive list.

Being aware of what you want will start to change your thinking and how you perceive the world and your life. You start to act — mindful, physical action that comes from your true potential and your true being. Being turns to focused action.

For me it became clear I wanted to write a book and become

a better speaker. I really had to push myself to stay accountable and committed to my daily habits towards these two goals - to take a cold shower, to start keeping a journal and so on.

When I started transforming myself I distanced myself from several people. I kept silent more often and listened more to my inner voice. This brought me a new state of energy and through meditation I learned to love myself, and stopped comparing myself to, or judging others. When we stop comparing ourselves with others and stop judging others we begin to experience true power.

We need to stop judging ourselves as well. Being harsh to oneself opens the door to insecurity. Insecurity is fuelled by unrealistic fears. You do not want to get into that anymore. We must walk up straight, chin up, square up our shoulders and, like Eckhart Tolle[28] says, *"Don't act, just be"*.

You are really something, something special

You really are one of a kind. No one else in this entire world is exactly like you. There are so many beautiful things about you. You are one of a kind, a treasure uniquely here in this space and time. You are here to shine in your own wonderful way sharing your smile in the best way you can and remembering all the time that your tiny light here makes a greater light everywhere.

You can, and you will contribute many wonders to the world. Show it. You have the qualities within you that many people would love to have. Remember everybody has qualities that make a person unique even though it seems that your qualities are not there or small to begin with. You have a big heart and a good sensitive soul. You were born like that. It's innate to all of us.

---

28. *Eckhart Tolle is widely recognised as one of the most original and inspiring spiritual teachers of our time. He travels and teaches throughout the world. He is the author of "The Power of Now" and "A New Earth".*

You are gifted with your own special thoughts and ways of seeing things. You know that life is not always played by the rules, but in the long run everything will work out just like that. You understand that you and your actions can turn anything around and that choices, once lost can always be found again. There is an inner reservoir of strength available in you. It is limitless, boundless even. I'd like to call this your resilience. It makes sure you will always get up and keep going come what may.

You have so many treasures within you which you are only now beginning to discover. And do not forget all the ones you are already aware of. Never forget what a treasure you are. That special person in the mirror may not always get to hear all the compliments you so sweetly deserve, but you are so worthy of such abundance of friendship, joy and love. Living your own purpose in your life will present you happiness. Happiness will bring you success.

"Forget about being nice, likeable, special, better than, free from, enlightened. Freedom isn't about becoming something, it is about losing everything. It's about giving everything back to the source which is who you are, it is about surrendering to yourself. And "yourself" is an absolute mystery. Yourself - your true self - is here, is free, is radically alive and present.

Do you dare to make "this" your altar, make "what is" your god? Or do you have to repetitively escape to thinking and imagining a future praying for salvation in some distant place that is always just slightly out of your grip?"

- Lisa Cairns[29]

---

29. *Lisa Cairns lives her life 'in love'. Lisa has been travelling the world giving talks and retreats in over 20 countries on the subject of Non-Duality and Oneness. She is author of the book "For the love of everything".*

The Law of Attraction

The Law of Attraction is one of the most important universal laws. It assists you in searching who you are, what you want and why you want it. The Law of Attraction is a universal law that states that similar forms of energy attract each other. Positive energy attracts more positivity and negative energy attracts more negativity. The Law of Attraction is based on the premise that vibrational frequencies (energy) tend to sync with similar frequencies. The Law of Attraction became popular through the movie "The Secret" in 2006. However, the principles of the Law of Attraction are mentioned in ancient scripts such as the Bible, the Tao Te Ching and the Emerald Tablet of Hermes ("The Secret" is based upon these scripts). The most successful people in history often make use of its theory. Napoleon Hill[30] conducted research by interviewing the five-hundred most influential Americans in his time. As a result, in 1937 he published his book "Think and Grow Rich" on the lessons he learned from Henry Ford, Thomas Edison, Albert Einstein, Theodore Roosevelt and many others. Now we have arrived in a time in which scientists (quantum physicists) begin to provide evidence that consciousness affects reality. In simple words, we can describe the Law of Attraction as like-attracts-like and dislike-attracts-dislike. That what you focus on will expand and materialise.

---

30. *Oliver Napoleon Hill (born October 26, 1883 – November 8, 1970) was an American self-help author. He is known best for his book Think and Grow Rich (1937) which is among the 10 best-selling self-help books of all time*

Exercise

Living your own purpose in life shows you and others your vibration. A positive vibration attracts positive vibration. Happiness will arise. Happiness that will bring you success. Here are three questions to find your own purpose;

1. Will you start asking yourself why you are here? What do you want? Where do you want to go? What do you want to accomplish?

2. Why do you want it?

3. What kind of feeling do you want to have?

Chapter VII

Finding your soul mate

"Someone can be madly in love with you and still not be ready. They can love you in a way you've never been loved before and still not join you on the bridge. And whatever their reasons, you must leave. Because you never ever have to inspire anyone to meet you on the bridge. You never ever have to convince someone to do the work to be ready. There is more extraordinary love, more love that you have never seen, out here in this wide and wild universe. And there is the love that will be ready."

- Nayyirah Waheed[31]

Why Women Cry?

A little boy asked his mother, *"Why are you crying?"*

"Because I'm a woman," she told him.

"I don't understand," he said.

His mom just hugged him and said, *"And you never will."*

31 Nayyirah Waheed is U.S. based writer. She began writing at the tender age of 11 after a teacher assigned an assignment that required the class to write a poem to put into a community newspaper. From that assignment, Nayyirah discovered a new medium for self-expression. From the age of 11 till now, Nayyirah Waheed has blossomed into a powerful poet/artist and woman.

Later the little boy asked his father, *"Why does mother seem to cry for no reason?"*

"All women cry for no reason", was all that his dad could say.

The little boy grew up and became a man, still wondering why women cry. Finally, he put in a call to God. When God got on the phone, he asked, *"God, why do women cry so easily?"*

God said: *"When I made the woman she had to be special. I made her shoulders strong enough to carry the weight of the world, yet gentle enough to give comfort. I gave her an inner strength to endure childbirth and the rejection that many times comes from her children. I gave her a hardness that allows her to keep going when everyone else gives up and take care of her family through sickness and fatigue without complaining. I gave her the sensitivity to love her children under all circumstances, even when her child has hurt her very badly.*

I gave her strength to carry her husband through his faults and fashioned her from his rib to protect his heart. I gave her wisdom to know that a good husband never hurts his wife, but sometimes tests her strengths and her resolve to stand beside him unfalteringly. And finally, I gave her a tear to shed. This is hers exclusively to use whenever it is needed."

"You see my son," said God, *"the beauty of a woman is not in the clothes she wears, the figure she carries, or the way she combs her hair. The beauty of a woman must be seen in her eyes because that is the doorway to her heart - the place where love resides."*

~ Author Unknown ~

"The secret", applying self-love on a path to meet your soul mate

In "The Secret", the movie[32] from 2006 in which a lot of wonderful things were portrayed about the Law of Attraction lies the

---

32. *The Secret is a best-selling 2006 self-help book by Rhonda Byrne, based on the earlier film of the same name. It is based on the law of attraction which claims that thoughts can change the world directly.*

key in finding your soul mate. Adding to that I would like to point out a few things about the magic of love and how strong love can be. I mention "The Secret" because it is a shortcut to manifesting your desires and to see what you want in life. It is about the Law of Attraction and the different universal laws.

How to create magical love?

A lot of us are disappointed in love. Some of us are wondering why is it we do not experience great love. I see many individuals of forty years and older who are utterly disappointed and do not believe in love anymore. They say their hearts are burned and were broken, damaged as it has been, but how can your heart burn and break!? It's of course as manner of speaking. It is 'only' the emotion and your feeling. And if you are sending your emotions and your thoughts to this direction, of course you get disappointed. When you have these thoughts, your actions line up with them and you will get the same outcome over and over again. Hence you will be more and more disappointed.

After my divorce I felt like this. My thoughts often saddened me, as I was paying attention to them, feeding them all the time. I felt sorrow about the situation. The only way for me was to talk about it and tell everyone how hard, difficult and terrible the situation was. I shouted from the roof tops. Wrong message though!

Guess what – I received more of this because I sent out negative thoughts to the universe. Love doesn't make you unhappy. Your thoughts make you unhappy, especially when you hold on to them. You consider them to be the truth. You consider them to be solid. Hard as a rock. Like I did. It is only energy passing by. Nothing more.

Truly, sometimes you can feel unhappy when the kind of love you experience is not what you were looking for. Feeling unhappy is a feeling. It is not something to wallow in. Feel it and move on. In the end you will understand that it wasn't real love or that it was just a negative feeling passing by. Real love is not changeable. It is constant and perseverant. Love embraces your sadness as well as your joy. Know that in true love you are never alone, always complete and one. In times of suffering and in times of joy. Inclusiveness makes the real love complete.

Changes and exploration

We change and transform our whole life. I can give you so many examples. For instance, I am in love with somebody and yet the other day we had an argument. What do you think, does this mean that the love is over? To cite another instance or another example somebody gives you some service and he or she expects the same from you in return. Will you stop liking each other if the favour is not returned? Or do you do the complete opposite and take everything for granted? What is the magical strength of real love? Let's explore.

When my daughters were born, I really felt inner strength and unconditional love. It's like a feeling you cannot describe. It is overwhelming. All you experience is being fine and feeling perfect. For me it was the most wonderful moment. While raising my children I fed them, I dressed them and I watched the miracle of them standing up and taking their first steps; making their world immensely bigger than before. I taught them their first steps on this planet, to grow and to be an independent person. A person who is happy and loved. My love for them grew day by day. It became stronger and stronger and so deep.

I remember when I was young with a six-year older brother and an eight-year older sister; my mom saw me as a special gemstone, a shining diamond. I was the rebel of the family. Good friends of my parents told me that they also loved me the most. They said I was special and moreover because I was born in Egypt made it even more special for them. This special something, this sunshine in myself also gave me something that I really wanted to share with the entire world. Something each and every one possesses within. Something, anyway in my case, that's connected with the old scarab, the mythological beetle from ancient Egypt.

As I remember my mother, she loved us all the same. She had not learned about inner-love yet. My mother loved us very much and she loved us unconditionally in her own way. She told me once: *'I can't love somebody except you, your brother and your sister because I don't love myself and I never will'*. Self-love for her did not exist. I did not say anything knowing I could not change her thoughts at that moment.

Is love based only on expectations? Do you love somebody because you are expecting something in return? Expectations are what you believe and desire. This kind of love is not real and not magical. You will treat love like it is something to negotiate about, nourishing the if-you-do-this-I-will-do-that mechanism. Or if-you-don't-do-this-I-will-not-do-that. True love is constantly present and unchangeable, from within. From the previous chapter you learned how you can love yourself and the steps to connect with alongside the insights of not loving yourself.

Inner power of love

We as people can change ourselves. We as people are here on this planet for a brief period of time. Our soul however is infinite. Many times though, people tell me: you're still the same, you did not change one bit. They are however not conscious about what they are talking about. Of course, I changed, because we change all the time. When we are at the age of two, we discover the world. When we are at puberty we change dramatically, physically and mentally. We change when we are twenty, forty, even when we are eighty. We constantly change, our thoughts, feelings and beliefs change. Everything is constantly moving and changing. Our body keeps changing all the time as well. For instance, your complete skeleton is renewed[33] every seven to ten years.

The real love of everybody is to step into the inner mystical side of love. The love that is innate. Those who experience mystical love by

---

33. *Your Body Is Younger Than You Think*- source: *https://www.nytimes.com*, 2005

breaking through the limiting thoughts of our past, by tapping into the innateness of our being, do not talk about it. Or talk only a little. These kinds of individuals are authentic. They dare to show their beauty. These people do more out of love. They contribute to the world by creating that which changes the lives of others. They are the creators of a better world.

Love is like a diamond

I go back to this special story that my mother told me in which she described me as the sunshine of the family. It's like that special ring with that gorgeous diamond you get from your loving partner. I have got one as well. When I look at it, it's for me something maybe materialistic, but constant. Because this stone will hold its shape and form, its beauty forever. This stone itself is unchangeable and so is the magical strength of love. The same counts for your soul. Cherishing and nurturing them will make them both even more beautiful and shiny.

You know that the magic of two people in love is not in the name of love, it's in the lasting connection two souls make. How about if you are sick or broke? Does the love disappear? What's the poetry and music of love you want to create? How do you express love?

For instance, I love singing. That is why it's quite easy for me too express love and to express my emotions, how I feel. When you realise that love is the reason and subject of your heart, you are heading in the right direction. This love also must be fed. It's like the relationship between a garden and its gardener. A loving gardener will be rewarded with the best harvest each year. I love my own garden. I love my brother's garden. I love my sister's garden. I nurture and cherish these relationships with them and it keeps growing.

When your own garden gets enough water and sunshine at the right time and everything grows in the right fertile soil, seeds will sprout and they will become beautiful flowers and plants. It's the same with the human heart, any human heart.

The love within us is always there. Just like the sun, the wind, the rain, the tides, gravity, seasons, they are always there, and they keep coming back. The sun brings you warmth, the rain brings you water. This keeps repeating itself. That is why your heart cannot be broken. It's like life itself. Everything comes, and everything goes. The dynamic is always there. It will never disappear.

Finding your soul mate

There is a chance in your life when you are open to it that you are blessed with meeting your soul mate. It can cause a restless and sometimes confusing feeling because it is a connection that is different from what you are used to. There are no words to describe what such a connection entail.

It's a magical form of energy, an intuitive feeling where everything is just right. Often, finding a soulmate occurs unexpectedly. Sometimes even at inconvenient moments, but nothing is further from the truth. It's like meeting someone for the first time, but in your heart, it feels like you have known each other for years. This is different. This is real.

Intimacy (even before the first kiss) is indescribable and if you look at each other, it feels as if you can see what the other is feeling at that very moment. Soulmates are people who get the best out of you. They are a perfect match because they are perfect for you even with all your imperfections. You respect and trust each other completely. You walk around with a big smile all day long. A smile that makes you feel complete. Complete because you have already processed your past and have created inner peace. The peace you radiate works like a magnet for each other and for your environment. Everyone wants to know your secret. It's as if you can take handle on the rest of the world.

When I had a date with my soul mate it did not matter what

I was doing that day-drowning in work, crunching to hit deadlines, helping my child doing her homework, juggling family commitments, packing and moving boxes, exhausted, struggling with some trauma, sleep deprived, coming down with a cold–if I had a hot date with my soul mate on the calendar? I would move heaven and earth and infinite galaxies to show up for that date. On time. Looking mighty fine. No resistance. No excuses. No complaints. Nothing could stop me from being with him. Get out of the way now!

How do you recognise your soulmate?[34]

If your partner is your soulmate then there is a chance that he or she has been around in earlier life stages. You can even get a sense of déjà vu as if the moment had already taken place somewhere else, maybe a long time ago.

Ever encountered two people who finish each other's sentences? Understanding each other's word games? Sending messages to each other at the same time? And if you first meet each other you notice that you have the same taste in furniture? Soulmates often have a mental indivisible connection that is comparable to twins. Look at couples on a terrace. What's their nonverbal attitude, their body language? Do they have the same bodily rhythm? Often you do not even have to hear what they are saying. You take one look and in a split second you know it is great or you know it is a disaster.

You will also fall in love with his or her flaws. No relationship is perfect and even soulmates will have their ups and downs. And yet, that connection is much harder to break. It's a lot easier for soulmates to accept each other's imperfections, to love them even. John Legend[35] calls it the "perfect imperfections". Sometimes it may be frightening that there is nothing that bothers you.

Soul mates see their relationship very often as "us against the

---

34 *Various books and websites are available on the subject of finding your soulmate.*

world". They feel so connected that they are ready and willing to challenge every aspect of life if they have their soul mate on their side. Because of your soul mate, you feel like there is a guardian angel next to you. It's not someone who consciously or unconsciously responds to your uncertainties. It's someone who is unconsciously competent in compensating your uncertainties. Soulmates go through thick and thin for each other. They will do everything for their partner.

A soul mate is not someone you easily walk away from. You can't imagine that you will ever be without him or her. They are someone you believe is worth fighting for.

Soul mates tend to look each other in the eyes more often and longer than ordinary couples when they talk to each other. This arises from a deep-rooted relationship between them. Looking at someone while talking shows a great deal of ease and trust.

How do you find your soulmate?

Your soulmate does not find you? You will be found, so be patient! And do not start searching for it yourself either. Believe me if you already think that a monastery is your best option, is because you've given up hope to find someone who will truly love you. At the same time if you secretly manifest what you really want and express or desire this wish, it will happen unexpectedly. Your inner peace must be present. That is a pre-condition. You must first love yourself to attract your soulmate.

Soulmates can be vulnerable just like that, it doesn't take any effort. Vulnerability is according to men something that belongs only to fragile women. This is not true. Only through vulnerability you become more powerful and you will become who you are. Luckily some men start to see this as well.

Soulmates do, feel and say the same thing at the same time. Say what

35 *Taken from "All of me" by John Legend, 2013*

you think now. It does not always have to be important things. Your brain also registers trivial things; a child that plays, a butterfly flying by, a text on a wall that makes you smile. You will see that your soulmate will probably register the same.

Process negative emotions and push them aside. Negative emotions lead to negativity. After all, what you think will happen. You create your own world with your own ideas. Negative people often create a negative life around themselves (you probably know people who complain about everything all day long). Positively tuned people radiate joy and love and will receive that back. One of the most negative emotions is jealousy. Often blindness arises from uncertainty or fear of losing your partner. The very uncertainty is often fed by insufficiently investment in each other. People are constantly comparing and thus creating the uncertainty in themselves.

The connection between soulmates is so strong that there is no room for jealousy. They are strong and stable within themselves and have no room for comparison with the outside world. Where others are jealous, a soulmate will enjoy the interaction the partner has with other people. He or she will know that no other can reach that level of relationship; 100% trust.

Follow your heart! Of course, in addition to your heart also follow your brain and for some, your gut feeling should approve the relationship; but it's your heart that first gives the signal. Eventually; you become a better, more beautiful, happier and indescribable magnetic personality while your soulmate is by your side!

You have a very strong connection, a virtual rope. Regardless of where you are or even when you can't be together for a while, the rope is always there like a soul that is "everlasting".

Exercise finding your soulmate

Have you ever experienced the feeling of looking in the eyes of somebody without any judgment? Not even being aware of a first impression?

At the same not being aware of time and space at all?

And especially, did you feel free to say what you wanted to express. The expression as you truly are, naked like a new born baby filled with love?

Did you ever experience a long verbal as well as a nonverbal connection like a smooth dance on the floor of two souls?

It need not be a love relationship. It can also feel like the connection that twins quite often have. They even feel connected when they are thousands of miles apart.

Use your imagination and think of the moment(s) when you had such a feeling, that vibe. That twinkle everywhere in your body. That magic. That all-of-a-sudden-being-there-feeling.

Got it?

That moment you think of now, will shift your vibration. It will shift you into the familiar space within you, where your true self resides and naturally wants to be.

Connect with it.

Feel the unity.

Chapter VIII

Better sex after fifty

Love is a friendship set to music

- Joseph Campbell [36]

Sexual health is a state of physical, emotional, mental and social well-being in relation to sexuality. It is not merely the absence of disease, dysfunction or infirmity. Sexual health requires a positive and respectful approach to sexuality and sexual relationships as well as the possibility of having pleasurable and safe sexual experiences free of coercion, discrimination and violence. For sexual health to be attained and maintained the sexual rights of all person's must be respected protected and fulfilled.

- World Health Organisation 2006 -

When we get older, a lot of people really do not know what sex is, anymore. It seems that only for a small part of our life we are sexually active. After a certain age or because of one reason or another, sex becomes less important. Although, there are always exceptions, of course.

---

36 Joseph John Campbell (1904 – 1987) was an American mythologist who worked in comparative mythology and comparative religion. His work covers many aspects of the human experience. Campbell's magnum opus is his book The Hero with a Thousand Faces (1949).

However, always remember this; if you want your life to be a hot date, you must show up to it. Therefore, show up for intimacy as well. Show up for that special moment with your loved one. Being one while enjoying each other. Discovering more and more intimacy while souls merge.

When I've got children after we got married, I stayed the lady I was before, walking on high heels. Most women around me were and are still wondering how I can walk on them? I do not really care what they think. I just like to make myself attractive and beautiful. It feels good and comfortable. It feels like wearing a warm coat made just for me.

How do I stay attractive and beautiful? First of all, I accepted menopause and all its effects on my body and mood. If we fight it, it will become worse. Don't fight it. Although, it was hard, I was getting crazy in the beginning and wanted to take hormones (oestrogens). I took them for one week. I had to call my sister (she's a doctor) because I thought I was getting depressed. Of course, it was a side effect of the hormones. I stopped taking them immediately and learned to accept my situation instead. Yes, it is there and it is an inseparable part of the cycle of life. To me it was also one of the starting points of a new journey to exploring my own inner wisdom.

In the beginning of the 20th century women often were not aging beyond fifty and therefore menopause was hardly an issue back then. Nowadays people get older and stay active much longer. Enjoying sexual activity after fifty is great and it gives you more pleasure and satisfaction. Quite a lot of people stop being sexually active after they have had children. I talked to many couples confirming that it was a fact of (their) life. I remember being in that same state when I was quite often stressed as a young mother with children. Somehow, I could not seek my inner peace at that time let alone the time to make love.

Do we need some incentive or what?

We first start to change when we are 'hit' by something and then we feel we have reached the lowest point in our life. Or if we are inspired by some event, a walk-through nature, a powerful talk, a great film or a jaw dropping sunset; we might start to change. Do we need to sense some necessity or some external inspiration to even start to talk about our sexual problems with our partners or with our physician? Being and staying sexually active adds to the quality of your life, anybody's life.

Sex is a basic need (see Maslow hierarchy of needs in Chapter 3). Your whole bodily system therefore benefits from you performing the act of love. It even has an eminent effect on your longevity. Yes, it does. So show up for sex as well.

I can say that sexual activity and satisfaction after my menopause has been the best and has never been so good as it is now. I enjoy it, because there is no need to worry about getting pregnant for instance. There are no kids asking for attention. There is no big career move that needs to be pursued. There are no unfulfilled expectations anymore (no-more-how-it-should-be). There is only love. There are no past experiences to be dealt with. There is only the present to dive into. The present with all the infinite possibilities to explore.

How do you stay attractive after fifty?

How do you do it? How do you stay attractive? How can you stay like that, being fit, vital and radiant? Where do you get your energy from? I can answer these questions. I would love to.

My thoughts make my emotions. My emotions determine the direction of the day. They are the combination of energy and motion. They resonate with those who need the same vibe or with those who recognise this vibe since they are vibrant as well. Vibe-attracts-tribe.

Now, let me ask you. What do you think is the secret to being more attractive?

1. When I started to transform myself my first learning was about self-love. The more self-love you have, the more

attractive you are. I could nearly date myself! This could be the challenge for you. As soon as you reach this state of being and you want to date yourself, that is the moment you got it. In the past I always put myself in second or third place. Nowadays I really enjoy myself. I enjoy the silence. I enjoy being in nature and even walking alone. I love being by myself. I feel comfortable with myself. I feel vibrant.

2. What do you eat every day? Believe it or not, I sometimes eat junk food as well but more often I realise that we are what we eat. I'm aware of the food I eat every day. This knowledge helped me; eating refined and sugary food adds to the speed of acidifying your body. Acidification is the main reason for the aging of your cells and therefore your body. The more you acidify the quicker you age.

Do you eat a lot of fruit and vegetables? Do you drink enough water? Maybe with a bit of lemon in it? Do you take your vitamins each day? How do you feel? Do you feel vital and energetic? Is your energy level constant? Are you aware of those activities that give you energy and those that suck the energy out of you?

It doesn't matter if you are skinny or curvy, you must love and nurture your body and you must love your food have to feel great. Your food has to give you a great feeling and if food is giving you a great energetic lasting feeling you also get more energy. Do not be misguided by muesli fruit bars or energy drinks. Over 'sugared' food will make your blood sugar levels jump up and down. Keep away from refined food. It will wear you out in the long run.

People who have a constant energy level and experience vitality through the day by eating healthy food are more attractive and healthy. And of course, it is also the other way round; garbage-in-garbage-out. If you love yourself, you radiate. When you radiate, you can feel the response around you. People are giving you energy instead of sucking it out of you.

3. I always pay attention to my underwear. It's so important whether you're size XS or XL. You can seduce at any size. How do you feel when you wear some old ugly unattractive underwear? Or how do you feel when you wear some black lace seductive underwear? It is important even when you are in your menopause. Not only for women but for men as well, simply to avoid feeling that we do not need sex anymore.

   High heels, wear a dress instead of jeans, manicure, pedicure, nice hair – these are more examples of feeling attractive even after fifty. Life begins at fifty. A new era of self-discovery of your beauty and true self begins.

We need to cuddle and touch each other more often on an inner level. Instead a lot of people start to cheat or hide the truth from one another. It is so sad when you are married and having less or no sex nor intimacy.

Sexual health after fifty is more than ever important for our physical condition. You are more authentic and you are confident. Besides, knowing that you will live longer will become even more crucial to your health.

It is however quite common in our society that even though we will live longer, those aged fifty are still considered to be seniors or even named elderly people. It's weird to categorise people like that. We only recently discovered that we will live to be one hundred years old within about fifty to sixty years. We do not need fitness for 50+ people. We do not need to put labels on people. Humans aren't categories. We are complete and free individuals independent of what age we are.

If we are in a deep loving relationship we are transcendent in our sexual relationship. It's very important to experience deep intimacy, a deep connection, fully present, being in the moment. It is almost as if you are one while being two when making love. Do you recognise this? I sincerely hope so.

Vulnerability

Are you vulnerable? Vulnerability is a great force and an extraordinary start to deepen communication and connection. Vulnerability will present itself if you are in a deep loving relationship. You automatically start to play, experiment and explore each other while being so intimate.

Without communicating in a vulnerable way no relationship can succeed because in the beginning there is only passion. It's not love. You know it won't last forever. You have to invest in that extraordinary type of open and sincere communication in the first stages of your relationship to reach that intimate sexual experience. So, you should start to be less conservative (if you are like that) and talk more about it. Talking about and sharing your sexual needs and desires and being open to your partner can be the start of improving your mutual health and vitality.

Yes, I know and I hear you, it will probably freak you out. I did, when I started expressing my vulnerability. I was afraid I would be mocked or laughed at by my partner. And in the end, I would only feel deeply embarrassed. We all know too well we want to avoid the pain of being ashamed at all times. But I persevered; I did it, I stumbled, I fell, I tried once more and finally I got better at it. You can as well. You only need some willingness. The willingness that is already there inside you.

It will present you and your partner the same excitement and joy, your blood pressure will go down and you will feel more energetic during the day. To stay happy, cuddle each other, be sexually active, touch each other each day, compliment, be attentive, be receptive and be warm and caring. You will make each other happy because when you make your partner happy, you are as well. Happy-attracts-happy.

The Law of Allowing[37]

Like the Law of Attraction, the Law of Allowing is also important in our relationship.

You are out of alignment if you think that the other person needs to think and feel the same way as you think. Accept yourself as you are without inner criticism.

Let me illustrate this law with a story. Once upon a time a student was having a conversation with Anthony de Mello, a well-known Indian psychotherapist and priest. They were discussing the subject of 'helping others'. At a certain moment Anthony said, '*I always tried to help, but it didn't really work; so I quit doing that*'.

Of course, the student asked, '*But what is it that you do now?*'

Anthony replied, '*I rain*'.

The student responded with, '*Huhhhh?!*'

Anthony said; '*What I mean is that I'm completely there. Doing what I do. Being what I am. And I rain. Rain sometimes drops on fertile soil and immediately something starts to grow, rain sometimes falls on dry soil and then it makes the soil fertile for future growth and sometimes rain tumbles on a rock and nothing really happens then. And that's what it is. Some people love the rain, some people can't stand it. That's also what it is. What we can and allow ourselves to do is to show one self and to rain, just like that*'.

This is our nature. Be what we already are.

We cannot change gravity, we cannot turn the tide and we cannot change our true nature.

Our true nature of well-being, joy, peace, love and resilience.

Poured over by our DNA makes it what we are.

---

37. *The Tao of Allowing: Surfing on the Law of Attraction by GP Walsh, November 6,*

So allow yourself to express yourself completely.

Just like that.

Chapter IX

How to be happier after fifty

All happiness comes from desire for others to be happy.
All misery comes from the desire for oneself to be happy.

Shantideva [38]

You know there are certain myths about how we are doing during or after menopause. People prefer to avoid the subject or refuse to admit that some things have changed. But we know it is there, menopause for women and peno-pause for men. Both women and men experience a lot of changes. The internet is full of stories and examples.

What is our problem, then? The myth is we gain weight, we get depressed, we get a lot more wrinkles, we get mood swings, we get sleep disorders, we easily get fatigued, we get hot flushes, we fling things around our precious kitchen for no reason, we get pissed off if our husband is suddenly extremely nice and so on. The children leave the house and it seems we have lost a purpose in life. We lose control of our life and we have trouble concentrating on anything no matter what it is.

---

38. *Shantideva was an 8th-century Indian Buddhist monk and scholar at Nalanda. He was an adherent of the Madhyamaka philosophy of Nagarjuna.*

The myth is that menopause is the cause of all these things. But is that the truth? Is it not a lack of self-esteem which a lot of us start to experience upon noticing the first grey hair in the mirror? Is it not some sort of miserable resignation to the inevitable last years to our lives? However, everything that happens starts in our mind. One thought is enough to make things happen. Sure, your body undergoes a lot of hormonal changes, but it is not the cause for you feeling lousy, confused or disturbed.

When we are depressed we stop exercising and we start to eat junk food. By the way, it is also the other way around. We do not even think about healthy food or loving ourselves. Remember, everything starts with only one thought. Everything can be depicted as the infinity symbol ∞ which connects everything together, your mind-body-spirit. They are all connected, forever; it is a closed system. One thought affects everything, one bite of junk food affects your body. Experiencing joy affects your body. It's a magical thing. Be aware as such.

Everybody tells me that I should be a happy, happy woman because I am fortunate to have the right genes. Or so they say. They think I will look like this forever. Like someone ten years younger. So let me ask you; can I have 'happy' genes and still eat junk food? Yes, of course. Well I used to. During my transformation however, I realised that a major part of it is to dramatically change my eating habits. To learn a new habit, especially eating habits, is not easy but possible. Try to change one habit at a time, for instance start eating twice the amount of vegetables or replace sugared food and do so for at least forty days. You will start to shift your horizon.

With my tremendous shift forward I started to attend yoga classes, I changed my eating patterns, learned to really appreciate and love healthy food. Gradually I could eliminate prefabricated food. I love chocolates of course, but I prefer quality over quantity. Look at the ingredients of some cookies and chocolates (often containing a lot of sugar and lacking the amount of nutritious cocoa). Yes, I know, I have said it before and I will keep on doing it because the power of repetition should not be underestimated.

You are the only one who decides what you put in your mouth. You choose between feeling happier and content or staying miserable because of the sugar levels jumping up and down.

Where do all these decisions start? Of course, in your mind, with a single thought. Pleasure, pain, hot flashes, frustration, they all start as one thought. Everything starts in your own brain. This cannot be changed in a day, but it is part of a process. How my transformation benefitted me during and after my menopause and more pointers on how to be healthier can be found in the next chapter.

Accept that your age is just a number. Your mind makes you beautiful or ugly. Your thoughts make you either miserable or happy, before, during and after your menopause. Be aware of the power of a single thought and choose your thoughts wisely!

When I look at the statistics[39] in the Netherlands, I find it rather troubling that while people are enjoying more freedom than ever, there is a corresponding decline in well-being and an increase in depression. There are more and more people depressed. Statistics show that more than one million people in the Netherlands are depressed. In other western countries it is not much different. This means that one in every seventeen individuals is depressed. The statistics from 2016 show that people aged forty to forty-nine are most prone to depression. *How come, I ask?*

We live in one of the wealthiest countries in the world; people are free to do what they want, opportunities all around, one can earn enough money, abundance is everywhere you may think. People can enjoy themselves in numerous ways considering that the health system is one of the best in the world, the economy is stable; but somehow

39.   *https://www.cbs.nl/nl-nl/nieuws/2016/04/meer-dan-1-miljoen-nederlanders-had-depressie. The mission of CBS is to publish reliable and coherent statistical information which responds to the needs of Dutch society. The responsibility of CBS is twofold: firstly, to compile (official) national statistics and secondly to compile European (community) statistics.*

there is a high percentile of people in depression within this country. It is a critical mission to find out what it is that makes people happy and satisfied so that the number of depressed people will drop dramatically. Everyone can experience a lasting happy feeling. Happiness is the most powerful and the highest form of success in life.

The truth about expectations

I would like to talk about expectations. Do you know how expectations influence our daily life? Do you know that the expectations you have, once you let them go, will make you happier? Do you know that too many expectations lead only to more suffering? Do you know that the more expectations you have the more resistance you will experience? Expectations might be at the root cause of our depressions. Expectations are like if-I-do-this-I-will-get-that, and if not then I will be disappointed.

On the other hand, this nasty place of unfulfilled expectations delivered me a marvellous insight. The insight left me in awe. Suddenly I became aware of what I was doing. Let me share with you some of my own experiences coming from that nasty place. In the past I was always expecting that others would love me if I just loved them first. When I first came to the Netherlands, I was a different girl compared to who I am today. I came from a different culture where we had different behaviours, history, traditions, standards and values.

I felt disappointed that the love I gave I did not get in return. It made me less happy. I started to complain, nagging about it all the same. I started to suffer. I also thought that what I did in my country, I could prolong here in the Netherlands. I expected overnight success. I expected that my career in my previous country would be the same here. I was disappointed again. I thought that when I came here because of my husband that we would have permanent pleasure and joy. How disappointed I was when I faced with the reality of not having a job, of not having the same nice apartment I had in Prague, not having my parents or my friends around me and not hearing and speaking my mother tongue. I nagged a lot in those days. I was a pro at that. I suffered, until it hit me. I recognised what I was doing. Somehow unconsciously I stood still, took a deep look inside and discovered I had to turn things around. Turn myself in the direction of being receptive, open and available. Expressing affection, appreciation and warmth.

I want to point out how you can eliminate the expectations you have. How to let them go and to be happy again. When I started my transformation life, was not easy. I conquered a lot of challenges during my professional life in the Netherlands. I was bullied, but I did not realise that it was me and only me and my expectations. My expectations that other people would love me as I loved them. My expectations that other people would accept me unconditionally as I accepted them with an open mind. My expectations of my own ego and inner child crying because she did not get the sweets she wanted. I was a 'nagger'.

My sincerest advice is to use this formula; Stop – Watch – Start. It works magically. Each time one of your expectations is not met and therefore you notice a thought rising in your mind of not being good enough, of being disappointed, of being wrong, of being frustrated, notice what happens within yourself, and just stand still. Wait a while. STOP whatever you are doing. Only five seconds is required. Do not let anything come in between so that the thought may disappear. Just WATCH and be aware of what is going on. If you feel something, just feel it. If you learn something then you learn something. If you get some insight that leaves you in awe then you get an insight that leaves you in awe. If you sense something then just sense it. WATCH for only five seconds. And move on. Do what you want to do. Proceed. START. It helped me to stop being a 'nagger' and to start being 'IVA'. I - for inspiration, V - for Vibration and A - for Attraction.

This formula also applies to your friendships and relationship. Not long ago, my friendship with a few friends faded away and eventually ended. When people are changing, when you are reaching more success, when you are becoming the person you really are, you tend to lose your old patterns and of course you gain new ones. We are changing all the time. Nothing lasts forever. Because people change, you and I are evolving, our friendships evolve as well. What worked in the past does not always work well in the future. That is the unwritten rule of life.

If you are aware of the inevitable fact that some of your friendships will disappear and you will automatically gain new ones, you will be happy again. Happier because your pineal gland starts to open to a new earth, a new dimension, a new possibility. The mystic of the Egyptians and their third eye is one of the signs you are opening your pineal gland. The pineal gland is a tiny organ in the centre of the brain that plays a key role in 'Descartes'[40] philosophy. He regarded it as the principal seat of the soul and the place in which all our thoughts are formed. It is also the place where your intuition resides. You will notice that during your transformation you will let yourself be guided by your intuition. You learn to trust it. You learn to surrender to it. And of course, after being guided you use your common sense to be practical and put things in sensible and insanely beautiful actions. Actions that contribute to the lives of others. Actions that can forever change the lives of those near and dear ones.

---

40. *René Descartes was a French philosopher, mathematician, and scientist. Dubbed the father of modern western philosophy, much of subsequent Western philosophy is a response to his writings, which are studied closely to this day), best known for the quote from his Meditations de prima philosophia, or Meditations on First Philosophy (1641), "I think therefore I am," philosopher and mathematician Rene Descartes also devoted much of his*

Happiness is not destiny

What I also learned from my journey is to let go of the thought to be happy all the time. There are a lot of articles around now. It's a hype, "how to be happy this, how to be happy that". It's like you can get to some delightful spot or place. Do this and do that and then you will get to the Valhalla of Happiness. How about that for an expectation?!

People do not realise that they are looking for something outside themselves. Happiness is not out there. It's within. You were born with it. First you must regain clarity. Clarity about your vision of who you are. Stop with chasing happiness and look at yourself first. Look in the mirror. Who and what do you see?

When you look in the mirror, what can and will you say to yourself? Are you happy with yourself? Are you happy with your imperfections? Or are you constantly looking at others, admiring photo-shopped pictures in magazines? Do you envy the ones that look amazing? One of those body builders, or one of those beautiful skinny ladies with gorgeous hair? Don't be misled! Live your own life!

Also, happiness cannot be found in the perfect appearances of others or in the how-to-lists presented to you on how you should look, move or behave. When you realise you should let go to be happy all the time and stop expecting that other people (like your family) will love you as much as you love them, you will be happy. Don't expect overnight success, slowly you will start to be happier.

Ten tips how to be happy

These tips derived from my own journey of discovery is what really matters to be happy. Pick the one(s) that touch you. Pick the ones that make you feel alive.

In this life of ups and downs, being happy requires deliberate action guided by some pointers. It activates your happiness from within. Everybody deserves to be happy, but the reality is that only a few are truly happy. In this piece, I will be discussing some tips. They point to the core of happiness.

1. **Discover who you are.**

    The very core source of happiness comes from within. Therefore, you must discover what it is that brings you joy. Everybody has those unique happiness triggers. You may need to list them and stick to them. Yours may be to watch a football match or come up with a new recipe for your family to enjoy together. There is that thing that certainly makes you happy and you can only find them from within.

2. **Be with others who make you smile.**

    Life is too short for us to be surrounded by people who give us headaches or drain the energy right out of you. Build a network of people who make you happy. Most of the time these are people who share similar values. That can be a group of friends. In fact, you are most fortunate if you can find happiness in the circle of your family members.

3. **Hold on to your values.**

    Never compromise on your values. Nothing hurts you more than seeing the effect of compromising on your own values. On the other hand, if you stick to your guns; you will be the happiest person on earth. Your core value may be integrity;

you must hold on to it irrespective of the opposition. It will haunt you if you don't. Consequently, you will be unhappy. Hold on to your values. Oh, one other thing, do not push others in convincing them they should have the same values as yours. It sucks.

4. **Accept the good.**

   There are many things that are way beyond our reach in life. Some situations are just meant to go wrong notwithstanding our effort. Often, we are hurt and unhappy when things do not go our way. For us to be happy we need to accept the good and resolve not to bog our head with what we cannot change. Some things can be influenced directly by us, some things happen, just like that. This is the only way we can stay happy in life.

5. **Eat light and right.**

   Watch your diet and focus on healthy nutrition. This will affect your shape and physical structure. Consequently, when you stick to the right nutrition you will be happy with yourself. Remember the body-mind-spirit connection.

6. **Do things you love.**

   We find joy in the activities we engage in. Do not just pick up an employment for the sake of it. Resolve to do only those things that make you happy. At the end of the day, what really counts is not the volume of what we do, but the happiness we derive from what we do.

7. **Find purpose.**

   Life is all about contribution. Your purpose is that very contribution to humanity. Believe me, people that live in purpose live in fullness of joy. The joy contributing their part to humanity is unspeakable!

8. Listen to your heart.

The moment we disobey our hearts; we lose our peace. We are troubled. So to stay happy, listen to your heart. You'll know when it 'speaks'.

9. Push yourself, not others.

There are a few things we can change about ourselves. Don't even think of changing anyone else. The best you can do is to change yourself, and you will be amazed at the happiness that it brings you.

10. Imagine and visualise the best.

Be positive about everything. Imagine the best out of every situation. Have a 'Yes, and?' attitude. Always say yes first when you encounter anything. Eliminate 'Yes, but'. Thereby, you will be the happiest person all day.

I would like to end this paragraph with a proverb from Albert Einstein[41]:

"Imagination is more important than knowledge. Knowledge is limited. Imagination encircles the world."

41. *Albert Einstein (1879 – 1955) was a German-born theoretical physicist who developed the theory of relativity, one of the two pillars of modern physics (alongside quantum mechanics). His work is also known for its influence on the philosophy of science. He is best known by the general public for his mass–energy equivalence formula $E = mc^2$ (which has been dubbed "the world's most famous equation").*

Plants that will give you a great happy feeling

Aloe Vera – Egyptians would hang this at the door to remove the negativity and bad souls and bring new life and hope in their homes. This plant is meant to be for longevity and long life. Try to drink Aloe Vera or have this plant in your home.

Myrrh – is a plant of happiness and is used during Czech weddings. Everybody has myrrh in his jacket and or dress.

Bamboo – I have it in my garden and this plant brings positivity. It brings you clearness and awakens the greatness in you.

Basil – brings love, passion, wealth and happiness to your home. You can use it not only in your pasta as a pesto but also as a decoration in your kitchen or garden. It can also be used as an anti-depressive, antiseptic and antibacterial plant.

The Law of Trust
Trust = To Rely Unto the Spirit Totally

Trusting yourself is also one of the components of happiness. The affirmation from Buddha mentioned below illustrates it:

In reply to the question, what is the best that people can possess, what brings them the truest sense of happiness, what is the sweetest of the sweet, and what is the most pleasant life to live? The Buddha answered[42]:

"Trust is the best that people can possess; following the way brings happiness. Truth is the sweetest of the sweet; and the practice of insight is the pleasantest way to live."

You know that nothing bad can happen to you because you

---

42 *Source unknown*

have trust and you have the power within yourself. You trust yourself from within. It is much like self-love. It all begins with understanding and then loving yourself. In self-love you know that you can conquer anything and it does not matter if you are alone or with someone else. Because the more powerful you are, the stronger you are from within. You know that the world makes you more beautiful and you make the world more beautiful.

Exercise

Journaling

Write in a notebook (a nice one) for about 10 min each day, preferably in the morning when you wake up. Think of somebody or something you like. Something or somebody you feel good about. That something can also be the activity you love doing. Let your thoughts flow in the direction what feels good for you. Put it on paper.

You will notice after a while that your focus shifts. Your focus will be directed to beauty, joy, peace, gratefulness, creation and much more. Eventually you will focus less on things not being complete or perfect and realise that everything around you remain as perfect as can be.

Can you start to comprehend the meaning of this awareness?

It's truly awesome.

Chapter X

How to be healthier

Physical change: when I first became aware that something was starting to change in my body during my menopause I realised very quickly that I needed more vitamins and minerals. Often people ask me why I'm looking so young. I answer that I am taking vitamin E and vitamin C every day.

A lot of young people have trouble with cellulites. They lack vitamins in their body. If you do not expel the toxins from your body, they remain inside the cells of your body. For women they show in places such as your legs or your butt. It is true that some physical discomforts occur as we are getting older. Is it because we are getting older? Or has it to do with our eating pattern?

When I started paying attention to my eating behaviours, I realised that I was eating a lot of cookies and sugars. I realised that gaining weight during my menopause would not become a fact of life for me. A lot of women keep on eating the same old stuff every day. Sometimes however we realise it, but we find it hard to do something about it. We think it is part of getting older. It's all in the game. We tend to talk a lot about it because we still want to look good, but we still have one hand in the cookie jar. The only way to change this is to start changing those thoughts and slowly remove or change our eating patterns.

It took me more than two years to become vegetarian (not in a rigorous manner, I do cheat sometimes in guilty pleasures, but that's fine). It was a huge shift to stop eating meat, (although I still eat fish and dairy products). I started to remove toxins from my body and my pH level started to improve. The levels are usually bad due to the consumption of junk food, refined sugar and artificial additives. They speed up the acidification in your body which causes cells to age rapidly. It will take months if not years to remove these acids from your body. Vitamins such as A, B, C and E added with some specific minerals will dramatically support your physical condition and vitality especially when you are getting older.

What are these vitamins and minerals good for[43]?

Vitamin A

Vitamin A is very good against inflammation, bacterial infections and improves your eye-sight. It destroys free radicals and will give you smooth skin and reduce the appearance of wrinkles. You obtain it from eating carrots, spinach, some types of cheese, apricots - my favourite fruit - known from the proverb to have a skin like a peach. It is true you know. Vitamin A can also be found in fish, broccoli and melon.

Vitamin B

Vitamin B is very good for concentration and can be found in nuts. I eat some nuts each day. Have you ever looked at the shape of walnuts? They look like the brain. This is not some coincidence. These

From the National Centre for Complementary and Integrative Health - US Department of Health - https://nccih.nih.gov/health/vitamins

nuts contain B12 which is very good for the nervous system and B2 which is the engine of your cells. You will find vitamin B12 in fatty fish, spinach, yoghurt, chia seed and soya.

With B1 you will feel refreshed and awakened. I remember when I started my menopause I often felt fatigued. My hot flashes were fortunately seldom, but I started to experience tensions in my head. I took immediate action and changed my eating habits looking for vitamins and minerals which served me well. Take some of these pointers to heart as it may prove beneficial. There are good supplements of vitamin B you can use as I do especially during the winter months.

Biotin and Vitamin B5

Next to vitamin B, doctors suggest biotins as it is good for your skin and hair. As we tend to lose hair when we are get older, using biotin will postpone the effects. Biotin can be found in almonds, mushrooms, spinach, crab, carrots, liver and nuts. vitamin B5 also known as panthenol is good for us when we are starting to lose our concentration. It will protect your hair before it gets grey and it also improves your resistance against inflammation. It's also the vitamin that keeps you slender and slim. Don't use it too often but take it from time to time for a certain period if required and if you are losing more hair than normal.

Vitamin C, D and E

I think everybody knows that vitamin C and E not only protect you against illnesses, but they also make you happier and more responsive. It stimulates hormonal and other neural processes in the brain. Processes that will slow down while aging. It's like rebooting your brain with vitamin C and E.

Of course, vitamin C can be found in fruit but be wary that as you are getting older it is good advice to take some extra vitamin C and vitamin D. As we are getting aging, we lack vitamin D especially in those countries where there is hardly any sun in the winter. Lack of vitamin D causes calcium deficiency in your bones. Vitamin D can be found in fish such as salmon and sardines or in whole-wheat bread, but you can also buy it as a supplement.

Vitamin E is not only good for your heart as it contains healthy unsaturated fats, but it also supports your blood flow and transport of oxygen. That means your body will be given more oxygen which prevents cell degeneration. Hence eat almonds, walnuts and butter.

Forget counting calories but put your attention to natural food. Refined food or prepared food with more ingredients than needed or with too many additives can be harmful to your body. They can be the cause of many illnesses which again causes anxiety or even depression. Make it a habit to use Vitamins C and E every day.

Calcium, magnesium and other minerals

Next to vitamins there are also minerals such as calcium and magnesium. Magnesium is also good for your concentration and works well against fatigue. I often drink mineral water with magnesium. Most people lack magnesium in their body or diet, hence it is very useful to take it as a supplement: You can eat plenty of bananas or blueberries, but you have to eat kilos of bananas to get the same amount as what you get from a supplement. There are also other minerals like ferum to carry more oxygen in your blood and selenium which is good for your cells as well.

When you are getting older and you start to put your attention to food and your eating patterns, you will start to realise that to gain weight is really nonsense. There is a lot being written about emotional eating as well. A lot of things in our lives we do unconsciously most of the time, we do not realise it and we often fool ourselves when we say we gain weight from water for instance. Come on, are you kidding me?

In the previous chapter, I shared my concern about depression in the Netherlands. Food, however, can have a major impact on your mental health and certainly your well-being.

So, this made me wonder; what are the foods against depression and anxiety? Of course, food with lots of vitamin B12. You can get it from avocado and seaweed for instance. Studies[44] show that a deficit of vitamin B can cause depression.

Omega-3 can be found in fish or taken as a supplement and is also great for your mood. I prefer salmon as it is a fatty yet healthy fish and simply delicious. Don't forget seeds. Some of the seeds have lots of omega-3, chia for instance which is a small tiny black seed that looks like poppy.

I remember the time I spend with my grandmother and she always wanted to give me fish oil. I hated it and I was nearly vomiting when she gave it to me. Now I know it had a purpose, to feed my brain. Whole grains also contain vitamins B and are very good against depression. Eating white and refined grains and white bread is bad for your blood sugar. Many illnesses these days are caused by wrong food and by wrong eating patterns.

My morning ritual

Start each morning, for instance, with a squeezed lemon in lukewarm water and drink it. Your intestinal flora will thank you for it. Or if you want to have a detox day, take lukewarm water with lemon, cinnamon and a bit of honey. It's perfect to detoxify your body.

Then take your vitamins and your minerals. Take a cold shower! For me a cold shower is a new habit which I started lately to wake myself up. It's a wonderful way to fire up your system.

Best thing to eat in the morning is fruit. I prefer fruit because it is very light and it is healthy to take simple sugars in the morning. Fruit is my life-changing food. Let me share with you a wonderful smoothie I drink regularly; squeeze two oranges and put it in a blender together

---

44 *Vitamin B12 deficiency can be sneaky, harmful, a Harvard health publication - Harvard Medical School, January 10, 2013*

with a banana and a handful of spinach. I usually also add some ice cubes. It's a great drink.

Remember that it is not about how old you are, but how you feel about yourself. You are the only one who can change your life. Either something new comes into your life or something new comes out of you. What you put into your body also comes out. What do you choose right now? Garbage in - garbage out, or treasures in - treasures out? When you're enjoying your food, you are starting a huge shift in your mind. So start today and put only in your body what you want to be, feel it!

Tips for your health for a whole week

I would like to suggest that after you are dressed to take time for yourself. Try ten minutes of meditation to set the tone for the upcoming week or do some yoga or body exercises. Do not push it, just set the intention for the week.

Then on Monday, get up a bit earlier. Instead of smashing the clock and fall asleep again, falling into the trap of the 'snooze rhythm'; start your week more energised, relaxed and happier, of course.

Take a cold shower, you are used to it now; aren't you? And write down at least three things that you are grateful for. Do this every day.

Start with journaling. On my desk I have a To-do list for that specific day. Not all things are important for that day, but it helps me to get organised even if I can only complete it the day after or even next week. Yet, it is very important to journal about what you want to do and should do. It reduces stress and stressful situations because your tasks are written down. It gives you an immediate overview of your activities and clears your mind. It also forces your imagination.

Don't wait for the moment of flow, the moment you are in a good mood or the moment you will get some 'a-ha Erlebnis'. Turn this kind of journaling into a weekly routine. And then everything will go smoothly. You are in a flow.

Ones or twice a week, you can take a nice walk outside or go to the gym or take dance classes or learn a new language. To empower and improve your brain after fifty; it is vital to stay alive, active and to improve yourself all the time. Never stop learning.

It does not matter what kind of hobby or other kind of activity you do; just activate and train your muscles and brain, and your blood pressure will go down.

Spend more time with your family, partner and or your friend(s) as it is very important to sustain and improve your intimacy. Not only the relationship with your partner but also your relationships with your friends and family. It's important to focus on your family issues and not only your work issues.

"You know we are all actors", as Shakespeare[45] once said, *"but all of us are playing the role very differently"*. It is important not to play but to be authentic, or as what Joseph Campbell once said: *"The privilege of a lifetime is being who you are"*.

Go out and have fun, watch the sea or enjoy nature, go to a concert, see a movie or go to a museum.

---

45 Taken from "All the world's a stage" by William Shakespeare

How to feel better immediately?

I would like to share some easy tips on how you can feel better instantly. Life, at times, is like a roller coaster and sometimes it is like a silent sea. Sometimes it is even like very stormy and rough sea.

What are the physical, yet simple steps that you can apply each day to empower you instantly and bring you happiness in your life?

What about jumping, what about being a child for a while? When you go for a walk or on your way to work or even when you're at work, just jump. You can also sing when you are jumping and think about a sunny beach or another beautiful place in your memory. When you are singing you cannot be angry. Just try it. Most likely your feelings are not as bad as you thought after singing. And if somebody is listening, who cares? It's about you and only you. Music is food for the soul.

Open your photo album or your smart phone and look at your favourite picture of your partner or a picture from your holiday. This brings a smile on your face again and it will give you renewed energy.

What is your favourite smell? Do you like perfume or do you like essential oils? It can bring you a happy feeling. When you are frustrated or when you are stressed, use lavender. Lavender is great for preventing stress, it soothes you. I have a lot of lavender in my garden and I also got a lavender pillow in my bed. It brings me serenity.

Eat quark and drink kefir[46], which is a very old drink. Or eat Greek yogurt, which is a probiotic to improve your positive thoughts.

---

46 *Kefir or kephir alternatively milk kefir or búlgaros, is a fermented milk drink that originated in the Caucasus Mountains made with kefir "grains", a yeast/bacterial fermentation starter source: Wikipedia*

Law of Nature

Mind, body and soul are one system and are interconnected. They closely work together. They need each other. There is an even deeper connection. We, as humans, are all connected. It's like nature. In nature, we connect with ourselves again. As all people are connected, so are the trees in the forest. What we see is only a small percentage of the real us and/or the whole tree. The roots of the trees in the forest are deep and widely spread. They automatically connect with other roots of other trees. And it doesn't matter if the forest contains various kinds of trees. They keep connecting with each other. The same applies to people. There are differences between us, but we still stay connected while keeping our own individuality. And remember the examples of the butterfly and the feathers I mentioned previously? Animals in nature (when we pay attention to it) give us the signs we need at that moment in our life or in a specific situation.

Chapter XI

How to be successful?

"All the adversity I've had in my life, all the troubles and obstacles, have strengthened me... You may not realise it when it happens, but a kick in the teeth may be the best thing in the world for you."

- Walt Disney [47]

I have written several times in the past about the qualities and elements that successful people share, but I think perhaps the most important one is their ability to get past excuses. So many people in life get hung up on excuses - feeling they can't apply for that better job, start their own business, or take whatever risk because of whatever it might be.

Excuses are like noses, we all have one. But when you can train yourself to see these flimsy ideas for what they really are and stop treating them as a brick wall on your path, you can move past them and towards your own success. Become A-No-Excuses-Lady or A-No-Excuses-Gentleman!

---

47 *Walter Elias Disney (1901 – 1966) was an American entrepreneur, animator, voice actor and film producer. A pioneer of the American animation industry, he introduced several developments in the production of cartoons. As a film producer, Disney holds the record for most Academy Awards earned by an individual having won 22 Oscars.*

Here are just a few of the excuses I often hear. Whether from individuals about their own dreams or from executives about their company's direction.

1. **Don't have the money or the resources.**

    I have heard this at every level, from the one who has an idea to start his own business and all the way up to the mega-corporations I have consulted. The point is you can make this excuse whether you've got one euro or one million.

    The people who get past it, however, are the ones who succeed. They find a way around it. They barter or trade for the services they need. They start a side hustle and save money. They cut their expenses. They find an investor, take out a loan, apply for a grant.

    Successful people do not let the lack of any resource (money being just one of them) keep them stuck for long.

2. **I do not have the time.**

    All successful people in the world like - Richard Branson, Bill Gates, Oprah Winfrey - have the same twenty-four hours in a day that you do.

    Examine closely how you spend your time and you will see where your priorities truly are. There are very few commitments in this life that are non-negotiable. Allowing yourself to fall into the trap of the idea that you do not have time to do what you want just shows that you do not want it badly enough. This is the same when you are holding yourself back in a relationship and find excuses for not having enough time.

3. **I've never done this before. I cannot change. Or I do not want to change.**

    There are loads of things you succeeded at, that you had

never done before until you tried it. You had never walked before you did, never driven a car before you first got behind the wheel, never had a job before your first one.

Every journey starts with the first step and you must take it. Our fear is the biggest enemy and hurdle for our own success.

4. I do not have the skills. I do not have enough talent.

I have one word of advice for you: Google.

You can find instructions, how-to and even books and courses on how to do practically anything on the Internet – for free. If you still cannot find what you need then buy a book. Still struggling? Hire a coach.

You can get a college-level education just from reading the books found in your local library, so throw away the idea that a fancy degree is standing between you and what you want, because it is almost never true.

5. The conditions aren't right. I am not at a right place. It's not the right moment.

Waiting for things to be perfect is perhaps the worst possible excuse. Because things will never be perfect. No one will come along with a stopwatch saying: "If you start NOW, you will succeed!"

Loads of things were launched at the "wrong" time or before the world was ready. Some of them failed and some succeeded beyond anybody's wildest dreams. Waiting for the "right conditions" is like the fisherman sitting on the banks waiting for the fish, but never sinking his hook in the water – that is to say, kind of pointless.

The truth is people are going to disagree with you. They won't get your vision. They would simply not have faith in you. However, only one person needs to believe in what you are doing when you start, and that is you.

6. **I do not have anything new.**

Some of the most successful businesses out there did not invent something totally new. Which came first, Living Social or Groupon? MySpace preceded Facebook.

The point is, you do not have to do something completely new to be successful. Take something that already exists and improve it, change it, tweak it, turn it around and give it your own spin.

There are millions of books out there, but each one is different. There are thousands of stand-up comedians each with his or her own show. Loads of accountants, software developers, designers, manufacturers, engineers et cetera.

It is not about whether you are unique, but rather how you will be different. What excuses have you heard? Or maybe you have an excuse that has held you back from success?

Do we sabotage ourselves?

Do we sabotage ourselves? We all make our own resolutions at the beginning of the year. For instance; we want to lose weight, we want to start a business, we want to spend more time with family or we want to start a vegan diet. What I find remarkable is when I pass by the shops in January they offer an extensive range of diet stuff, supplements and so on. In February, everything is gone. The next year, all of it is repeated. Why is that? As if only these periods are meant to change something? It seems hard to change our behaviour.

Self-love is the key to easily adapt new habits. Do not let neuroscientists and psychologists misguide you. They claim that only 5% of the people who try to change their habits will succeed within a period of three years. The other 95% have already given up. This knowledge suits the businesses focused on providing you with all kinds of plans for dieting, fitness, happiness, love fulfilment et cetera.

We are sabotaging ourselves, sabotaging from our own goal and our own success. Self-sabotaging is a combination of negative thoughts, feelings, actions and behaviours. And usually it is caused by low self-esteem and low self-confidence. We say we are okay, but we are not. Why are we doing this? It's comfortable to say I'm okay. If you are not okay, you are, somehow, not fitting in somebody else's expectations.

If we cannot reach our goals or objectives, there is usually a lack of desire, lack of decision, lack of belief or lack of support. Especially in my situation. In the past, I thought I could do everything by myself. I never asked for support. Why didn't I ask for support? When I started reaching out to others, I started to transform rapidly. The law of attraction directed me to the right individuals and I encountered more and more coincidences. Things coincided suddenly. It's like everything synchronised. When I started to see 11:11 (the number 11 is a symbol that indicates consciousness is trying to find its balance - left and right brain is being used at the same time), I realised, I was on my path of transformation. I discovered everything was possible.

We are all creators of our life. We always have the power of choice. We also have the power to choose what we think about ourselves. If you want to transform your life into a success and make your dreams a reality you must learn to reprogram your thoughts and keep them positive. 'I am' - are two of the most powerful words and the words you put after 'I am' determines your reality. So, if you say I am wonderful, I am great, I am lovable, I am beautiful, how wonderful does it sound? Moreover, how does it make you feel?

Most people are like monkeys. If the carrot is not sweet enough (not-enough-WOW) or if they are not struck hard enough by setbacks (not-enough-OUCH), they will not move. It causes a lot of pain and that is why it is better to live an unconscious life. Do we desire things in our life or are we only living from one day to another?

When I passed fifty and I started to follow classes and studied the law of attraction, I started to re-program my mind. Of course, it's a very painful process to go through. It's a process in which I was tossed back and forth between - I am okay and will stay like this forever against my entire life where I will repeat what I am doing as if I am a robot - and I will start to design my dream life and take specific steps to commit fully to it and persist in doing so.

Look at all the possibilities. First, we must clarify what we are saying to ourselves when we proclaim that we do not want to gain weight, we do not want to be fat, we do not want to get wrinkles and we do not want to be ugly and old. If you do so, you are telling the universe, of course, that you want to be ugly and old, that you want to gain weight, that you want to be fat and so on and forth, the universe will respond to that accordingly. The universe cannot know the word 'not' as it only responds to the possibilities. Therefore, the universe will also support you when you shift your thoughts into what you wish for, what you desire to be or become. Be wise in choosing your words.

I have a very big dream where this book of mine will be successful. I have no idea if it will be, but the desire is there. I want to inspire people. Not only do I wish to see that I have made it abroad as an extraordinary Czech girl who, despite having lived in a communistic era, has managed to raise two beautiful daughters as a single mother alongside an illustrious career.

When we see men of worth,
We should think of equalling them;
When we see men of a contrary character,
We should turn inward and examine ourselves.

- Confucius 48

---

48 Confucius (551 B.C. – 479 B.C.) was a Chinese social philosopher, whose teachings deeply influenced East Asian life and thought - https://en.wikiquote.org/wiki/Confucius

Why this desire; the desire to inspire others?

I was inspired by a story. A story from a book written by Wallace D. Wattles[49] , 'The science of getting rich'. He tells the story of a young boy playing the piano who suddenly gets really upset. The piano teacher asks him, *'Why are you upset just like that?'* He says, *'I can hear the music inside me, but I can't make my hands go right.'* The music inside of him is the urge of original substance containing all the possibilities of life. These possibilities of life live in each one of us. Possibilities that want to be expressed in living our dreams. Your dreams. Therefore, the dreams you have are infinite seeking to express itself through you. So, what are your big dreams?

Don't tell me or others that you will keep on living your unconscious life even when you're already over fifty. Accomplish your dream. Put it into action. It does not matter if it's a small dream or a big dream. It differs from person to person. It's your life, it's your choice, it's your own happiness; and no one else's.

The Law of Dharma[50] – The Law of Success

This law is about your life mission. When you ask yourself what's your life mission, what are you thinking about? Do you know your 'what' and do you know your 'why'? And do you also know the 'why of your what'?

The Law of Dharma has three components:

The first component is 'who I am' which is your real identity. When

---

49 Wallace Delois Wattles (1860–1911) was an American author. His writing has been widely quoted and remains in print in the New Thought and self-help movements. Wattles' best-known work is a 1903 book called The Science of Getting Rich in which he explains how to become wealthy - source Wikipedia. The book 'The science of getting rich' is based on Hindu Philosophies that say, "One is All", The movie "The Secret" which mainlined the term Law of Attraction and the idea that your thoughts shape your destiny was based on this book of Wallace D. Wattles. In the preface of his book, Wattles explains how he has "sacrificed all other considerations to plainness and simplicity of style".

50 The Seven Spiritual Laws of Success: A practical guide to the fulfilment of your dreams

you say, 'I am' and you put words behind 'I am'; that is what you truly are. Think about it. Say it out loud. No excuses, anymore.

The second component of the law of dharma is to look closely at the unique talents you possess. I have heard a lot of people say that they have no talents. Some people in response to the question even told me that they are fortunate to be so talented. And some people say that they have too many talents and have become arrogant or narcissistic. No matter what people say, simply remember that you are unique and you have your own talents. It does not matter if you studied or not. It is easy to find out what your talents are. Just write them down. Make three categories; work – hobbies – other activities and write down the skills and knowledge you have in those categories. Put it away for a while and add to it later. You will notice your list to be extensive. Especially if you believe you are alright, if you believe you are worthwhile and if and only if you truly love yourself.

The third component is important. When you slowly lose your ego, you will begin to ask others *'How can I help you?'* You will start to ask, *'How can I be of service to others in need?' 'How can I contribute?'*. Everybody has a life mission. Everybody has talents. Ask yourself how you can be of purpose to others (start an inner dialogue with your soul). Do not ask yourself how you can earn a lot of money first (considering that is an inner dialogue dominated by your ego). When I started to apply this component in my life, miracles started to occur. I am sure it will do the same for you.

Exercise

This exercise is good for positive thinking and banishes negative thoughts.

As mentioned in chapter one, "the law of seed", you can see every belief as a seed of thought. Belief is the origin of thoughts. Our mind is full of these seeds, positive ones and negative ones. When we are in silence we start to learn how to sort these seeds. Fertilizing the positive and destroying the negative. Practicing this while meditating or when in silence or while practicing yoga will make you start noticing the very nature of these seeds like a gardener does. You will recognise those who need nurturing and those that need no attention. Those that get the attention, will flourish. Those that do not get the attention, will vanish. This is your starting point to achieve success in life. So, put your attention where it is needed for you to experience prosperity.

Chapter XII

How to become wealthier, my tips as a single mum

"I find it fascinating that most people plan their vacations with better care than they plan their lives.
Perhaps that is because escape is easier than change."

- Jim Rohn [51]

When I came to the Netherlands I only had one hundred Dutch guilders and at that time I did not realise how my career would evolve. *Where am I going?* I had no idea about my dreams, I had no idea about my goals. I noticed that not a lot of people had any savings or at least used their cash to make some smart (long-term) investments. Don't get me wrong, there were probably a lot of people with savings, but nobody used their savings. Not even a part of it, for buying a house for example. People however had huge mortgages and nobody realised that their houses were actually owned by the bank. A house that could easily be claimed by that bank if things would go wrong financially.

The crisis starting in 2007 was a cultivating result of the seeds many people planted without weeding from time to time, without

51. *Emanuel James "Jim" Rohn (1930 – 2009) was an American entrepreneur, author and motivational speaker. He mentored Tony Robbins - source Wikipedia.*

keeping track of it, without taking care of it. Unconsciously and blindly following what society seemingly wanted from us and told us. A cultural difference, for instance, was that the people in other countries needed a bit of savings of at least 10% to buy a house. Because of the tax advantages in the Netherlands, people could lend 110% of the purchase price of the house. When the crisis showed its ugly face, a lot of people were frustrated and had to sell their houses in despair.

This kind of insane spending of money can be prevented. It's not necessary because there are many smart ways to make sure you are wealthy and stay wealthy. Here are some tips how to deal with your wealth. I learned them as a single mum in times of crises and high unemployment.

It was time for me to choose. I asked myself what was more important for me back then. I asked myself if I wanted a life of joy, freedom and success or if I wanted a life of getting as much stuff as I wanted such as a house, a car (or two), lots of holidays and my own servants. I discovered I did not need a castle just to show off to my neighbours or friends. It would certainly not make me happy.

Now what would you choose? What comes first? Who is kidding who?

How to spend wisely?

Think about this.

When you take 100% as being your monthly income and then divide it in:

No more than 50% is for your mortgage and your other fixed bills such as gas, electricity, water, telephone, internet and insurance. So this should be 50% and no more! Look at your net salary and then at your monthly bills and compare. What do you notice?

So these bills will come every month as necessary costs.

Then 10% for savings. Yes, read carefully. Use 10% of your income to save. For me, it did not matter if I earned a lot or just a bit or if I was unemployed as I had been saving for a long time. At times, it was merely 5% but usually I put aside 10% of my net income.

Yes, I know. Nowadays, it is not profitable to save, but you should have that nice comfortable feeling of being able to live on your savings to "survive" if required.

This made me really very confident. Imagine your washing machine breaks down or if you suddenly want to or need to go on an adventurous vacation or you are confronted with other unexpected expenses. Your savings are therefore very important as well.

We arrive at 60%. What would be the next 10%?

Of course, your education and development. All the time we are evolving and we are changing! It doesn't matter if you follow some four-year program or a two-day course or study books or essays or learn a new language or learn how to make furniture. Lifelong learning is very important.

Up to the next 15%. I used to go out or do wonderful things with my family. Going to a restaurant, a zoo, some attraction. And so, we arrive at 85%.

The next 10% you can invest in real estate or other investments such as antiques, art or whatever suits you. Your hobbies too if you wish. But do not invest what you borrow! If you lose this 10% there is no problem at all. Do not spend more than 10%.

The last 5% you can use for charity or other unexpected things.

Summarizing;

50% mortgage/rent, gas, electricity, water, internet, telephone and insurance.

10% savings.

10% education and books.

15% pleasure.

10% investments.

5% charity or unexpected.

Did you know this? Did you know this is how your expenses are spread over several distinct categories? Do you see it as a wise decision to do so?

It's crucial to organise and structure your household. It gives you a clear overview. It gives you peace of mind. It teaches you what to do to keep it under control. You need this knowledge and being conscious about it gathers the possibility to live a free and awesome life.

Ten things mentally strong people do

In my opinion, your mental health is fundamental to your wealth. Not only your physical vitality is important, your mental resilience and adaptability is just as equally important. Mentally strong people (it doesn't matter how many challenges they went through) are usually the inspirators, the guiders, the helpers and the savers of so many lives.

What is it that mentally strong people do? First of all, they move on. They move on and this very aspect is key especially if you want to be mentally strong as well, you will have to move on. It does not matter where you are right now, it does not matter what kind of feelings you have, it does not matter if you are in grief right now and it does not matter in what kind of situation you are.

My mother always told me: it doesn't matter how many times you fall down but the most important is that you will stand up again. It isn't about falling, it is always about getting up again. So, remember mentally strong people do not waste time feeling sorry for themselves. Of course, you need to take some time to recover, learn your lesson and after that stand up and move on.

Secondly mentally strong people do not give away their power.

Remember what Sir Winston Churchill said: 'Never Ever Give Up'[52] And the same counts for; never ever give away your power. I was tempted to do this. All the times I wanted to say "no" but I still did not, being busy pleasing others and forgetting myself.

The most challenging of moving abroad for me from one day to another was that I had to start all over again right from the beginning. Now I know that not giving away your power and keeping control about yourself makes you mentally strong. It's far easier for me to say "No" now and to say "Yes" to myself.

Embracing your change is the third one. Welcome challenges, those that confront you with inevitable setbacks and those that confront you in testing your creativity. Those two might be presented to you at the same time. Our whole life we face challenges. Some of us face small and some of us face huge challenges. It only depends on how we respond to these challenges. Whether they will become huge or remain small? What are our responses now to these challenges? And what will they be in the near future?

This story illustrates how to deal with a seemingly unsolved situation in a creative manner;

A wealthy landlady was so proud of a valuable and gorgeous vase that she decided to have her whole bedroom painted in the same colour. Several painters tried to match the shade, but none of them came close to satisfy the eccentric lady. Eventually a painter approached her being confident he could mix the proper colour. And he did. The lady was really pleased with the result and because of that the painter became famous. Years later he retired and turned the business over to his son. *"Dad,"* said the son, *"there is something I've got to know. How did you get those walls to match that vase so perfectly?"* *"Son"*, the father replied, *"I painted the vase"*.

---

52 *'never give in, never, never, never, never—in nothing, great or small, large or petty—never give in except to convictions of honour and good sense.'* - *Churchill said this on the 29th of October 1941 in a speech at the school he attended as a boy, Harrow School just outside of Central London.*

You know that the conflicts in our mind and the setbacks we face are inevitable. Life is like that. Life tends to do its own thing no matter what. When we do not want to face them or try to avoid them we hide our inner shadow and it makes us more insecure and more weak. It also destroys our creativity and our bravery. It puts a thick fog over it. And thus, being blinded we cannot pounce on the opportunities which were always there.

The fourth one: Mentally strong people also stay happy. They do not complain and they are not negative. They do not waste energy with such people. They do not waste energy with things that do not matter in their life.

The fifth one: Mentally strong people are kind, sincere, warm, receptive, appreciative and authentic. They do not go out of their ways to please other people. I am writing this because I wanted everybody to like me. Of course, it had to do with my past. It had to do with my experience with communism. It was caused by the political situation, caused by my father losing everything, caused by all the struggling I had to go through. We lived in fear. As most of us live in fear instead of love.

I also learnt what has been told to us and what was taught to us at school. We had to shut up, not to speak up, just obey and behave. Of course, when you start to please everybody you are losing yourself little by little and you are getting weak. Mentally strong people invest their energy in the present. They do not dwell on the past. Are you dwelling on the past all the time? I know a lot of people do and sometimes my ego wants to catch me and it's trying everything to drag me back into that very same past. And it sucks. It sucks the energy out of me. Recognise this?

It's a huge shift to change your thoughts in the present moment. My mother lived in the past. All the time she was talking about the past. At the end I almost could not bear to listen anymore. I started to interrupt her and tried to shift her thoughts. She did not want that. The trauma was huge. There was a seed in her that was never weeded nor healed.

The sixth one: Mentally strong people also take full responsibility for their past behaviour. They do not hide for it by reproducing those stories in such a way that they will look good or avoid looking bad. I am not saying that my mother wasn't mentally strong, she was, but it was only seen on the surface. Her inner being was broken and was not to be healed.

The seventh one: Mentally strong people stop making the same mistakes repeatedly. They also celebrate other people successes. They do not know what the word jealousy, hate or fear even means.

The eighth one: Mentally strong people are also prepared to fail. They do not give up when they fail. Every failure is a chance to improve. They do not consider failure as a personal defeat. They consider failures as a sign they are doing the challenging work to show their talents. Obsessively passionate people make a lot of mistakes whereas lazy and indifferent people never make mistakes nor budge.

The ninth one: Mentally strong people also enjoy their time alone. They do not fear being alone.

The tenth one: Mentally strong people also do not expect immediate result. They celebrate the small steps. The Law of Attraction says that if you want to stay in your power, it's not wise to spend your time in the 'I want' place over and over again. Instead visualise that you are already there as you already have it. Don´t spend time on unproductive thoughts. Replace negative thoughts with positive ones.

The Law of Deliberate Creation

If you already read about the Law of Attraction and you understand the law, you can also practise the law of deliberate creation. This law relates to the Law of Attraction as well. In other words, if you choose your thoughts consciously, you attract that what you give some thought to. The law of attraction is like a boomerang. The law of deliberate creation adds consciously to your vibrations by making plans. Plans that activate your being into tangible manifestations.

Remember that creation makes us not only wealthier but also happier. When we compete, we can win or lose, when we create we gain and we become wealthier. From that state of being and focus on "to have it all" already makes you a happy healthy and wealthy human being.

I would like to be known as an intelligent woman, a courageous woman, a loving woman, a woman who teaches by being.

-Maya Angelou [53]

53 *Maya Angelou born Marguerite Annie Johnson; (1928 – 2014) was an American poet, singer, memoirist, and civil rights activist. She published seven autobiographies, three books of essays, several books of poetry and was credited with a list of plays, movies, and television shows spanning over 50 years. She received dozens of awards and more than 50 honorary degrees. Angelou is best known for her series of seven autobiographies which focus on her childhood and early adult experiences. The first, I Know Why the Caged Bird Sings (1969), tells of her life up to the age of 17 and brought her international recognition and acclaim.*

EPILOGUE

The cave you fear to enter, holds the treasure you seek.

Joseph Campbell –

Three Gods meet on a hill top.

They know a secret. The most important secret. The secret of life. The sort of secret every human being should know. The key to a happy, loving and prosperous life.

The Gods however do not want to give it away for free just like that. They want people to put some effort in finding it. It is a great journey to find such a treasure and to really embrace it.

One God says; *"Let's hide it on the highest mountain top on this planet, people will never find it, just because there simply isn't enough oxygen to even survive there for a few minutes"*.

But the others do not agree. People will become more and more inventive and will think of ways to survive under those circumstances.

Another God says; *"Let us hide it in the deepest spot we can find at the bottom of the ocean. Humans can't get there since there are no submarines yet that are able to dive that deep"*.

The other Gods do not agree. That will also be solved by people eventually. They will find a way.

The third God says: *"I know the best place to hide the secret. Let's hide it in people themselves. They will never think of searching there!"*

And so they did.

....

I told you about your gold mine at the start of this book. Did you find it? Did you find your treasures? Did you have to dig deep? You know you did. You´ve come all this way. And now it´s time to share it with the world. Time to shine and radiate like a lighthouse. Would you like to share your treasures with me?

I would love to hear them.

The journey

My life was a breath-taking journey, yet more is to come.

When I look back on writing my book I discovered my journey was quite like the journey Joseph Campbell described in his famous book 'The Hero's Journey'[1] . He describes twelve steps just like the chapters in my book. It describes the steps of transformation. It describes the steps of my inner journey.

To give you an overview these are the twelve steps.

1. Egypt and my birth; this is the starting point for everybody.

2. Adventure camel trip, pyramids, rag doll purpose; we usually follow the trap of society and following the status quo like everybody does.

3. Return to Czechoslovakia; fears, resistance, insecurities.

4. Life in communism; life in fear, but on the other hand life in happiness because of the unknown

5. Abortion, emigration to the Netherlands; inner voyage and external adventure.

6. Divorce; discovery of the unknown.

7. Single-mum-abroad-test, allot, enemies; what should I do.

8. Bullying, discrimination, laid off; the most difficult part for

---

1. *A quick summary of The Hero's Journey stages by Joseph Campbell van be found on Youtube: https://www.youtube.com/watch?v=GNPcefZKmZ0*

a hero.

9. Survival, seeing the light, personal development; the reward.

10. Everlasting learning; the road back.

11. Return to where everything started; resurrection.

12. Fulfilment; the circle is complete, sharing the message and knowledge (self-love and law of attraction), returning to the 'Ordinary World', continuous transformation, living in truth.

It took me fifty years to get there!

I hope you realize it doesn't have to take all those years.

Certainly, after you've read this short story;

An old Indian taught his grandson some lessons about life and happiness.

He said; *"Within us a struggle is going on, it's a fight between two wolves. One wolf is a bad wolf. He believes in anger, jealousy, greed, arrogance, guilt, revenge, lies, false pride, superiority and ego"*.

He continued: *"The other wolf is the good wolf. He stands for joy, peace, love, hope, humility, kindness, generosity and compassion. Within you the same battle is going on, and for all humans it's the same battle"*.

The grandson thought about it for a while and asked; *"But grandpa, which wolf wins the battle?"*

The old Indian smiled and replied: *"The one you feed will win the fight"*.

Love,

Iva